Black Authors and
Illustrators
of Children's Books

GARLAND REFERENCE LIBRARY
OF THE HUMANITIES   (VOL. 660)

Black Authors
and Illustrators of
Children's Books

A Biographical Dictionary
by BARBARA ROLLOCK

GARLAND PUBLISHING, INC.

NEW YORK & LONDON ▪ 1988

Library of Congress Cataloging-in-Publication Data

Rollock, Barbara.
  Black authors and illustrators of children's books.

  (Garland reference library of the humanities ;
vol. 660)
  Bibliography: p.
  1. Children's literature—Black authors—Bio-
bibliography. 2. Children's literature, American—
Afro-American authors—Bio-bibliography. 3. Afro-
American authors—Biography—Dictionaries. 4. Authors,
Black—Biography—Dictionaries. 5. Artists, Black—
Biography—Dictionaries. 6. Illustrated books,
Children's—Bio-bibliography. 7. Afro-American
artists—Biography—Dictionaries. I. Title.
II. Series.
Z1037.R63 1988   011′.62′08996073   87-25748
[PN1009.A1]
ISBN 0-8240-8580-9 (alk. paper)

Cover design by Renata Gomes

Illustration for title page from Ray Charles *by Sharon Bell Mathis,
Illustrated by George Ford (Thomas Y. Crowell Book).
Illustrations copyright © 1973 by George Ford.*

Printed on acid-free, 250-year-life paper
MANUFACTURED IN THE UNITED STATES OF AMERICA

Contents

Acknowledgments

I wish to acknowledge gratefully the help of Linda Garraud who started the preparation of the manuscript, Angeline Moscatt of the Central Children's Room in The New York Public Library, Margaret Coughlin of the Library of Congress, William C. Morris of Harper & Row, Lauren Wohl of Macmillan, J. Smilow of Scholastic, Norma Gulyos of the Brooklyn Public Library, and the many authors who responded by phone or letter to my queries.

Barbara Rollock

Introduction

Prior to the 1960s the names of few black authors and illustrators of books for children were to be found in popular biographical sources or library reference books. Since then more names have appeared, with emphasis on the few who have achieved some prominence because of the volume of their published work or the awards they have received. Earlier citations featured only the same few well-known authors: James Weldon Johnson, Paul Laurence Dunbar, Langston Hughes, or Arna Bontemps. The fact that many more blacks in the United States and elsewhere have made contributions to children's literature was overlooked. Their works can provide an integral study of the black creative presence in children's books.

The books produced by those indigenous to a certain culture represent an important guide and resource in understanding the aspirations, thoughts, and viewpoints of that people. When books are neglected, both adults and children who need positive role models or awareness of a view other than the stereotypical one given by the media are deprived of a valuable insight into the true identity of a given group.

The biographical sketches included in this book of authors and illustrators are presented to acquaint all children with some creators of children's books. Their works have been published in the United States, they may live and work in this country, Africa, Canada, or Great Britain, and they happen to be black. Bibliographies are provided that include a selection of the author's or illustrator's works, and may list some out-of-print titles by contemporary authors—many of these books have had short publication lives even though they may have represented a significant breakthrough at the time of their appearance. The works of authors or illustrators now deceased are also included if they lived in the twentieth century, and particularly if their work has had some historical impact on the literature.

A few of the authors and illustrators in this book are listed even when they chose not to write on black themes or on the black experience. The criteria for selection does not exclude, for example, an illustrator like Donald Crews, whose graphic art form appeals to a general audience and is within the common everyday experience of all children. The only exclusions are those authors known primarily for adult books who have written only one book for children: James Baldwin's *Little Man, Little Man: A Story of Childhood* (Dial, 1977); Owen Dodson's *Boy at the Window* (Farrar, Straus, 1951; Reprint 1972); Pearl Bailey's *Duey's Tale* (Harcourt, 1975); and Katherine Dunham's *Kasamance: A Fantasy* (Third Press, 1974) come to mind. Bill Cosby's cartoon-like books about Fat Albert are also omitted in spite of their popularity.

On the other hand, those whose publications have not been widely popular are included because the writer or illustrator had some great impact on children's literature. Works with original subject matter and quality literary style that have been issued by trade publishers have been preferred for selection. Edited works of interest to children and textbook materials are often cited, as well as books for older children or young adults.

Some may argue that this dictionary isolates rather than integrates talented authors and illustrators. The intention is to provide those ill-informed or curious about the subject with a single reference volume in which the works of black authors and artists are recognized in relation to their particular contributions to children's literature.

The dictionary is arranged alphabetically by the author's and illustrator's surname. A selected bibliography appears at the end of each biographical sketch. Titles known to be out of print are followed by the abbreviation "o. p." Photographs of many of the artists are included. I hope that this dictionary will heighten awareness of and perhaps foster an appreciation for those authors and illustrators little-known to child readers.

The biographical sketches reveal a range and depth of competencies, backgrounds, and experiences these people have brought to their children's books. A total of 115 sketches are included. Though many more have written or produced books for children in this century, the task of personally contacting authors and artists or finding adequate material about them has limited the scope of the dictionary. At this point, however, the names selected and listed represent those black authors who have made or are making literary history in the world of children's books.

Barbara Rollock
May 1987

Bibliographical Sources and References

Adams, Russell L. *Great Negroes Past and Present*. Illustrated by Eugene P. Ross, Jr. 3rd Ed. Chicago: Afro-American Publishing Company, 1981.

Colby, Vineta, Ed. *World Authors, 1975-1980*. New York: H. W. Wilson, 1985.

Dictionary of Literary Biography: Afro-American Fiction Writers After 1955. Detroit: Gale Research Company, 1984.

Evory, Ann, Ed. *Contemporary Authors: A Bio-Bibliographical Guide*. Detroit: Gale Research Company, 1982.

Herbeck, Donald E., Ed. *Caribbean Writers: A Bio-Bibliographical-Critical Encyclopedia*. Washington, D.C.: Three Continents Press, 1977.

Kingman, Lee, Grace Allen Hogarth and Harriet Quimby, Eds. *Illustrators of Children's Books, 1967-76*. Boston: Horn Book, 1978.

Kirkpatrick, D. L., Ed. *Twentieth-Century Children's Writers*. Preface by Naomi Lewis. 2nd Ed. New York: St. Martin's Press, 1983.

Klein, Leonard S. et al., Eds. *Encyclopedia of World Literature in the 20th Century*. 1st Rev. Ed. New York: F. Ungar Publishing Co., 1985.

Logan, Rayford U. and Michael R. Winston, Eds. *Dictionary of American Negro Biography*. 1st Ed. New York: W. W. Norton & Company, 1982.

Matney, William C., Ed. *Who's Who Among Black Americans*. 4th Ed. Lake Forest, Ill.: Educational Communications, 1985.

Meltzer, Milton, Ed. *The Black Americans: A History In Their Own Words, 1619–1983.* New York: T. Y. Crowell, 1984.

O'Brien, John, Ed. *Interviews with Black Writers.* New York: Liveright, 1973.

Preiss, Byron, Ed. *The Art of Leo and Diane Dillon.* New York: Ballantine Books, 1981.

Rush, Theresa Gunnels, Ed. *Black American Writers Past and Present.* Metuchen, N. J.: Scarecrow Press, 1975.

Schockley, Ann Allen and Sue P. Chandler, Eds. *Living Black American Authors: A Biographical Directory.* New York: R. R. Bowker Company, 1973.

Ward, Martha and Dorothy A. Marquardt, Eds. *Authors of Books for Young People.* Supplement to the Second Edition. Metuchen, N. J.: Scarecrow Press, 1979.

Zell, Hans M. et al., Eds. *A New Reader's Guide to African Literature.* New York: Africana Publishing, Inc., 1983.

Abdul, Raoul (1929-)
AUTHOR

The author/musician was born in Cleveland, and attended the Academy of Music and Dramatic Arts in Vienna. He pursued additional studies at Harvard University in 1966. Besides giving lieder recitals in Austria, Germany, Holland, and the United States, he was a frequent guest on radio and television and appeared in operatic roles in the United States. He has lectured widely in the United States: the Performing Arts Center in Washington, D.C.; Lincoln Center for the Performing Arts in New York, the University of Connecticut, Howard University, and Columbia University.

Among his awards are the Harold Jackson Memorial Award, the Distinguished Service Award from the National Association of Negro Musicians, and a key to the city of Cleveland. He founded the Coffee Concert Series in Harlem and has served on the faculty of the Harlem School of the Arts. He was secretary and editorial assistant to the late Langston Hughes and is presently the music critic for the *Amersterdam News*.

Bibliography:
The Magic of Black Poetry. Dodd, 1972.
Famous Black Entertainers of Today. Dodd, 1974.

Achebe, Chinua
[Albert Chinualumogu] (1930-)
AUTHOR

Most of the English-speaking school children of Africa are familiar with the works of this Nigerian author, whose novels are often adapted for publication in secondary school texts. His narrative combines folk tale themes and traditional African proverbs and gives glimpses of the cultural traditions unique to the Igbo people of Nigeria. Best-known in the United States is his work *How the Leopard Got His Claws*. *The Drum*, also recognized in English-speaking countries, was originally written in Igbo, and draws from a popular West African folk tale about a magic drum.

Achebe has held a variety of positions: teacher, editor, and university professor both in Nigeria and the United States. His publishing experience dates back to 1962 when he was Founding Editor of the Heinemann African Writers Series. He has also been director of Heinemann Educational Books in Nigeria and Naranife Publishers.

His awards include a Rockefeller Fellowship in 1960; a Nigerian Merit Award in 1979; the Commonwealth Poetry Prize in 1973; and doctorates in literature from Dartmouth College in 1972, the University of Nigeria in 1981, and the University of Kent in 1982. He was made an Honorary Member of the American Academy in 1982.

Bibliography:

How the Leopard Got His Claws by Chinua Achebe and John Iroaganachi, illustrated by Per Christiansen. Third Press, 1973.

The Drum illustrated by John Roper Eniga. Fourth Dimension, 1977 (o.p.).

Arkhurst, Joyce [Cooper] (1921-)
AUTHOR

Arkhurst is a librarian. Born in Seattle, she graduated from the University of Washington and Columbia University's School of Library Service. She has worked in the New York Public Library as a children's librarian and as a librarian in the New Lincoln School. She has also worked in Elizabeth Irvin High School in connection with the Little Red Schoolhouse, been a community coordinator in the Chicago Public Library, and developed a program at the Children's Neighborhood Center.

As the wife of diplomat Frederick Arkhurst, former Ghana ambassador to the United Nations, she has traveled to Ethiopia, France, Ghana, and West Africa, where she collected many folk tales. She currently lives in New York and is employed in the New York City public school system.

Bibliography:

The Adventures of Spider. Little, Brown, 1964.

More Adventures of Spider. Scholastic, 1971.

Baker, Augusta [Braxston] (1911-)
AUTHOR

"John Kennedy said, 'Children are the world's most valuable resource and its best hope for the future'. It is my hope that the public library will recognize this statement and will give its best service to the children and will support the librarians who are giving their best to tomorrow's library users."

These words identify Baker's principal interest. Well-known for her storytelling skills, Augusta Baker, a librarian, was educated at the State University of New York in Albany where she received her A.B. and B.S. in Library Science. Born in Baltimore, she began her library career in the New York Public Library in 1937. While working as a children's librarian in the 135th Street branch, she began the James Weldon Johnson Memorial Collection of Children's Books About Negro Life and its accompanying bibliography. The bibliography's title changed in 1971 to *The Black Experience in Children's Books*.

Although she spent thirty-seven years in The New York Public Library as a librarian—rising in the ranks from a branch children's librarian to Coordinator of Children's Services—Baker was also a popular lecturer and adjunct faculty member at Columbia University, Rutgers University, and the University of Southern Nevada, and a library consultant and organizer in Trinidad. Upon her retirement from The New York Public Library, she became Storyteller-in-Residence at the University of South Carolina in Columbia.

Among her many awards and honors are the first Dutton-Macrae Award in 1953 for advanced study in work with children; *Parents* Magazine Medal in 1966 for outstanding service to the nation's children; the American Library Association's Grolier Award in 1968 for outstanding achievement in guiding and stimulating children's reading; the Clarence Day Award in 1974; the Constance Lindsay Skinner Award in 1981 from the Women's National Book Association; the Regina Medal in 1981 from the Catholic Library Association; a Distinguished Alumni Award in 1975 from State University of New York at Albany; and an Honorary Doctorate in 1980 from St. John's University.

Baker is co-author with Ellin Greene, *Storytelling, Art and Technique* (Bowker, 1977). The widow of James Baker, Augusta Baker has a son, James Baker III, and is married to Gordon Alexander.

Bibliography:

The Young Years: Anthology of Children's Literature edited by Augusta Baker. Parents, 1950 (o.p.).

The Talking Tree. Lippincott, 1955 (o.p.).

The Golden Lynx. Lippincott, 1960 (o.p.).

Barnett, Moneta (1922-1976)
ILLUSTRATOR

Daughter of a tailor, the artist lived in Brooklyn and attended Cooper Union and the Brooklyn Museum Art School. From 1966 until her death she illustrated at least one book a year.

Bibliography:

Fly Jimmy Fly! by Walter Dean Myers. Putnam, 1974.

Sister by Eloise Greenfield. Crowell, 1974.

Me and Neesie by Eloise Greenfield. Crowell, 1975.

Eliza's Daddy by Ianthe Thomas. Harcourt, 1976.

First Pink Light by Eloise Greenfield. Crowell, 1976.

My Brother Fine With Me by Lucille Clifton. Holt, 1970.

Bearden, Romare H. (1914-)
ILLUSTRATOR

Bearden was born in Charlotte, North Carolina, but grew up in New York and Pittsburgh. The distinguished painter exhibited no interest in drawing until high school. He earned his bachelor's degree in mathematics at New York University, and later studied at the Art Students League under teacher George Grosz. Bearden went to Paris to continue study in painting and in the 1960s began his collages on black themes. In 1977, the Museum of Modern Art in New York held a major exhibition of his work.

He was art director of the Harlem Cultural Council and a founder of Cinque Gallery in New York for beginning black artists.

Bibliography:

Six Black Masters of American Art by Romare Bearden and Henry Henderson. Doubleday/Zenith, 1972.

Poems from Africa selected by Samuel Allen. Crowell, 1973.

Bennett, Lerone, Jr. (1928-)
AUTHOR

Lerone Bennett, Jr., was born in Clarksdale, Mississippi, and attended public school in Jackson. He graduated from Morehouse College in 1949 with an A.B. degree followed by honorary degrees: Wilberforce University (Doctor of Humanities) in 1977, Morehouse College (Doctor of Letters) in 1965, and Marquette University in 1979.

Bennett started his career in journalism as a reporter in 1949 on the *Atlanta Daily World*. In 1952 he became the City Editor of that newspaper. He became Associate Editor of *Jet* magazine in 1953, a year later Associate Editor of *Ebony* magazine through 1957, and then Senior Editor of *Ebony* from 1958 to the present.

He was Visiting Professor of History at Northwestern University in 1968-1969 and Senior Fellow, Institute of the Black World in 1969.

In addition to his honorary degrees, Bennett has been honored by the Windy City Press Club for outstanding magazine writing (1965) and has received the Capital Press Club's Journalism Achievement Award (1963); the Patron Saints Award; the Society of Midland Authors Award for *What Manner of Man* (1964); and the Literature Award, American Academy of Arts and Letters (1978).

Bennett serves on the Boards of Trustees at Morehouse College; Martin Luther King, Jr., Memorial Center; WTTW; and Chicago Public Television, and is a member of the Executive Council, Association for the Study of Afro-American Life and History, and Phi Beta Kappa, among others. He has also served on the National Advisory Commission on Civil Disorders, and attended the Second World Festival of Black and African Art in Nigeria as a delegate.

His books and short stories have been translated into

French, German, Japanese, Swedish, Russian and Arabic. He has traveled widely in Europe and Africa.

The son of Lerone Bennett, Sr., and Alma (Reed) Bennett, he is married to Gloria Sylvester and has four children: Joy, Constance, Courtney, and Lerone III.

Bibliography:

What Manner of Man: A Biography of Martin Luther King, Jr. Johnson, 1964.

Before the Mayflower: A History of the Negro in America, 1619-1966. Revised Ed. Johnson, 1966.

Black Power, U.S.A.: The Human Side of Reconstruction, 1867-1877. Johnson, 1967.

Pioneers in Protest. Johnson, 1968.

Wade in the Water. Johnson, 1979.

Bible, Charles (1937-)
AUTHOR/ILLUSTRATOR

The artist was born in Waco, Texas, and attended San Francisco State College in 1966–1967, Pratt Institute, 1969–1970, and Queens College of the City University of New York, where he earned his bachelor's degree in 1976. He worked for various printing and publishing concerns and was art director for the Jamerson Printing Company in San Francisco from 1952–1954, holding the same position in San Mateo at the Amistad Litho Company from 1963–1969.

His exhibitions have appeared in universities, galleries, and museums in New York and California, including the New Muse Community Museum in Brooklyn.

Bible served in the United States Navy from 1954–1956. His memberships include the National Conference of Artists, where he was a regional director from 1975–1976; the College Art Association; the American Institute for Graphic Arts; Council for Interracial Books for Children; and the Queens College of the City University of New York Veteran's Association.

Bibliography:

Black Means by Barney Grossman with Gladys Groom and the pupils of P.S. 150, the Bronx, New York. Hill and Wang, 1970.

Spin a Soft Black Song: Poems for Children by Nikki Giovanni. Hill and Wang, 1971.

Hamdaani: A Traditional Tale from Zanzibar. Holt, 1977.

Jennifer's New Chair. Holt, 1978.

Bond, Jean Carey
AUTHOR

Bond has lived in Ghana; she worked for a state senator after graduating from Sarah Lawrence College. She has contributed articles and book reviews to *Freedomways* magazine.

Bibliography:

A Is for Africa. Watts, 1969.

Brown Is a Beautiful Color. Watts, 1969.

Bontemps, Arna Wendell (1902-1973)
AUTHOR

Arna Bontemps is considered to be one of the initiators of the Harlem Renaissance movement of the 1920s and 1930s. Bontemps was born in Alexandria, Louisiana, but his family moved while he was still very young to the West Coast where he attended Los Angeles public schools. He studied at the University of Southern California and graduated with honors from Pacific Union College of California in 1923. In 1926 he won the *Crisis* Magazine Prize, the Alexander Pushkin Prize in 1926-1927, and a Rosenwald Fellowship and Guggenheim Fellowship for creative writing in 1949-1950.

His career spanned three decades. He was Head Librarian and Publicity Director at Fisk University, a member of the Chicago Circle Campus's social service division at the University of Illinois in 1966, and served on the faculties of both the University of Illinois and Yale University.

Bontemps was a close friend of Langston Hughes and his co-author on the well-known anthology, *The Poetry of the Negro 1949-1970.*

Bibliography:

Golden Slippers. Harper, 1941.

The Story of George Washington Carver. Grosset, 1954 (o.p.).

Lonesome Boy. Houghton, 1955 (o.p.)

American Nego Poetry edited by Arna Bontemps. Hill and Wang, 1963.

Hold Fast to Dreams: Poems Old and New selected by Arna Bontemps. Follett, 1969.

Mr. Kelso's Lion. Lippincott, 1970 (o.p.).

100 Years of Negro Freedom. Dodd, 1961; Revised Ed. Greenwood, 1980.

Boyd, Candy Dawson (1946-)
AUTHOR

Candy Dawson was born in Chicago, the oldest of three children. She was raised by her mother, a school teacher, after her parents' divorce. In the 1960s the author worked with Dr. Martin Luther King, Jr. as a field staff worker for the Southern Christian Leadership Conference. She later taught school in Chicago and Berkeley and trained teachers and taught at Saint Mary's College. Boyd earned her bachelor's degree at Northeastern and Illinois State Universities; her master's degree at the University of California, Berkeley in 1978; and her Ph.D. in Education at Berkeley in 1982. Among her awards is an Honorable Mention for *Circle of Gold* by the Coretta Scott King Award Committee in 1985.

Candy Dawson Boyd is married to Robert Boyd and lives in San Pablo, California. She is currently an associate professor at Saint Mary's College's Graduate Department of Education.

Bibliography:

Circle of Gold. Scholastic, 1984.

Breadsticks and Blessing Places. Macmillan, 1985.

Charlie Pippin. Macmillan, 1987.

Brawley, Benjamin (1882-1939)

AUTHOR

Brawley was born in Columbia, South Carolina, where his father, Edward McKnight Brawley, was pastor of a local Baptist church and a teacher at Benedict College. Young Benjamin attended schools in Nashville and Petersburg, Virginia. He later entered Morehouse College where he received his first bachelor's degree. In 1907 he received a second A.B. from the University of Chicago, and the following year a master's degree from Harvard.

In 1927 he declined the Harmon Foundation's second-place award for excellence in education. In 1913 he published *A Short History of the American Negro*; throughout 1916 he published several essays, articles, and reviews on black culture, history and biography; and during the 1920s he published books on English literature. His biography of poet Paul Laurence Dunbar is outstanding, and his *A Social History of the American Negro* is still highly acclaimed.

Brawley was married to Hilda Damaris Prowd and died on February 1, 1939.

Bibliography:

Paul Laurence Dunbar: Poet of His People. University of North Carolina Press, 1936 (o.p.).

Negro Builders and Heroes. University of North Carolina Press, 1937 and 1965 (o.p.).

Breinburg, Petronella
[Bella Ashey or Mary Totham] (1927-)
AUTHOR

Breinburg was born in Paramaribo, Suriname, South America. In 1965, she received a Diploma in English from the City of London College. She attended Avery Mill Teachers College from 1969–1972 and Goldsmith College in London from 1972–1974. In Paramaribo she taught school but was also a factory worker, a postal clerk, and a nurses' aide. She worked as a volunteer for the Red Cross and Girls' Life Brigade in Suriname, lectured in creative writing, and was an outdoor storyteller in London. For about two years starting in 1972, she taught English part-time.

Her memberships include the Royal Society of Health, the Greenwich Playwright Circle, and the Poetry Circle. In 1962 she received an award from the Royal Society of Health and in 1972 was given an "honorary place" award from the Suriname Linguistic Bureau for her book *The Legend of Suriname*. Her picture book *My Brother Sean* was a runner-up for the Library Association of London Kate Greenaway Medal in 1974.

Bibliography:

Shawn Goes to School illustrated by Errol Lloyd. Crowell, 1973.

Tiger, Tinker and Me. Macmillan, 1974.

Shawn's Red Bike illustrated by Errol Lloyd. Crowell, 1976.

Brooks, Gwendolyn (1917-)
AUTHOR

Pulitzer Prize winner Brooks was born in Topeka and began writing verses at the age of seven. Her inspiration comes from poets James Weldon Johnson and Langston Hughes, whom she met in Chicago where she spent most of her childhood. Her first poem, *Eventide*, was published in *American Childhood*, a magazine for young people, when she was only thirteen. She started her own neighborhood newspaper. By seventeen she was a regular contributor to the *Chicago Defender*, where more than seventy-five of her poems and other writings appeared in its "Lights and Shadows" column.

In 1943 and 1944 she won first prize for poetry from the Mid-West Writers' Conference, and again in August 1945 for her book of verse, *A Street in Bronzeville*. She won the Pulitzer Prize in 1950, the first black to be so honored, for her second book, *Annie Allen*, and was named Poet Laureate of Illinois in 1977. She has lectured widely and taught at several colleges.

Bibliography:

Bronzeville Boys and Girls illustrated by Ronni Solbert. Harper, 1956.

Brown, Virginia Suggs¹ (1924-)
AUTHOR

Most of Brown's professional life has been spent as an elementary school teacher. She was Teacher-in-Charge of the Banneker Reading Clinic in the St. Louis public schools; an in-service teacher of remedial reading techniques at Harris Teachers College in St. Louis; a television teacher of reading for adults; a consultant in the Reading Institute College of the Virgin Islands, St. Thomas and St. Croix; and Director of Early Childhood Education, Webster Division, McGraw-Hill Book Company in 1966.

Brown has been a member of the International Reading Association, Association for Childhood Education, International and the National Association for the Education of Young Children. She received the National Council of Jewish Woman's Hannah G. Solomon Award for outstanding service to young children.

She married Charles F. Suggs and lived in St. Louis.

Bibliography:
Skyline Series:
Hidden Lookout. McGraw-Hill, 1965.
Watch Out for C. McGraw-Hill, 1965.
Who Cares? McGraw-Hill, 1965.
Out Jumped Abraham. McGraw-Hill, 1967.

Bryan, Ashley (1923-)
AUTHOR/ILLUSTRATOR

"Un pont de doucer les relie" ("A tender bridge connects them") is the way Ashley Bryan thinks of the connection between his interest in African art, folklore, and music and his storyteller's skill in his children's books. Bryan was born in New York and grew up in the Bronx where he attended public schools. He went to Cooper Union and majored in philosophy at Columbia University. He remembers starting to draw in kindergarten, illustrating books to give as gifts to childhood friends. In 1964 he illustrated *Moon, For What Do You Wait?*, poems from the Indian poet Tagore. It was the beginning of a long association with the Atheneum publishing house.

Bryan has taught school at Queens College of the City University of New York, Lafayette College, the Dalton School, and the Brooklyn Museum, and has worked closely with Head Start and other community programs. His one semester at Dartmouth College as Artist-in Residence resulted in his eventual appointment as a permanent faculty member and chairman of the art department.

He has illustrated several children's books as well as retold many folktales based on African, American or Caribbean lore. Among the many books he has illustrated he especially prizes his two volumes of spirituals.

Ashley Bryan has traveled to Africa, Europe, and Israel, and has lived for a time in France and Germany. His art work has been exhibited in one-man shows and his interest in Afro-American poets is evident in his lectures and recitations. His *Walk Together Children* was a 1974 American Library Association (ALA) Notable Book and his *Beat the Story Drum, Pum-Pum* was a 1980 ALA Notable Book. In

1981 his illustrations for the latter won the Coretta Scott King Award. He lives on a small island off the Maine coast where he makes puppets with beach objects.

Bibliography:

Moon For What Do You Wait? by Sir Rabindranath Tagore, illustrated by Ashley Bryan. Atheneum, 1964.

Ox of the Wonderful Horns and Other African Folktales. Atheneum, 1971.

Walk Together Children: Black American Spirituals. Volume One. Atheneum, 1974.

The Adventures of Aku. Atheneum, 1976.

The Dancing Granny retold and illustrated by A. Bryan. Atheneum, 1977.

I Greet the Dawn: Poems of Paul Laurence Dumbar. Atheneum, 1978.

Jethro and the Jumbie by Susan Copper, illustrated by Ashley Bryan. Atheneum, 1979.

Jim Flying High by Mari Evans, illustrated by Ashley Bryan. Doubleday, 1979.

Beat the Story Drum, Pum-Pum. Atheneum, 1980.

I'm Going to Sing: Black American Spirituals Volume Two. Atheneum, 1982.

The Cat's Purr. Atheneum, 1985.

Lion and the Ostrich Chicks and Other African Tales. Atheneum, 1986.

What a Morning! The Christmas Story in Black Spirituals selected and edited by John Langstaff. A Margaret K. McElderry Book/Macmillan, 1987.

Burroughs, Margaret Taylor G. (1917-)
AUTHOR

Burroughs was born in St. Rose, Louisiana, and educated at Chicago Teachers College and the Art Institute of Chicago, where she received her bachelor's and master's degree in education. She has taught in Chicago public schools, Kennedy King College, the Art Institute of Chicago, and Elmhurst College. Founder of the National Conference of Artists and a member of Phi Delta Kappa, Burroughs was awarded a fellowship from the National Endowment for Humanities and was an American Forum for African Study Fellow in 1968. She is married to Charles Gordon and has two children.

Bibliography:

Jasper the Drummin' Boy illustrated by Ted Lewin. Follett, Revised Ed. 1970.

Did You Feed My Cow? illustrated by DeVelasco. Follett, 1956, 1969.

Byard, Carole
ILLUSTRATOR

Byard was born in Atlantic City, studied at the Fleisher Art Memorial in Philadelphia, and graduated from the New York Phoenix School of Design. Her paintings are well-known and she has also done illustrations for magazines, film strips, and advertisements. She taught at the New York League of Girls and Women and the New York-Phoenix School of Design. Her exhibitions and one-woman shows have won several prizes. She now lives in New York.

Bibliography:

Under Christopher's Hat by Dorothy M. Callahan. Scribner's, 1972.

Africa Dream by Eloise Greenfield. John Day, 1977.

I Can Do It By Myself by Lessie Jones Little and Eloise Greenfield. Crowell, 1978.

Cornrows by Camile Yarbrough. Coward, 1979.

Three African Tales by Adjai Robinson. Putnam, 1979 (o.p.).

Grandmama's Joy by Eloise Greenfield. Collins, 1980.

Caines, Jeannette Franklin (1938-)
AUTHOR

Caines grew up in Harlem. She has been active in organizations such as the Salvation Army, where she served on the board of directors. She is also a member of Negro Business and Professional Women of Nassau County and a Councilwoman of Christ Lutheran Church, Nassau County. She lives on Long Island with her husband and two children, and is currently employed at a major publishing house.

Bibliography:

Daddy illustrated by Ronald Himler. Harper, 1977.

Window Wishing illustrated by Kevin Brooks. Harper, 1981.

Just Us Women illustrated by Pat Cummings. Harper, 1982. Reprint. Trophy, 1984.

Abby illustrated by Steven Kellogg. Harper, 1973. Reprint. Trophy, 1984.

Chilly Stomach, illustrated by Pat Cummings. Harper, 1986.

Campbell, Barbara (1939-)
AUTHOR

Campbell was born in Arkansas but lived in St. Louis as a child. She earned her bachelor's degree at the University of California in Los Angeles. She was a reporter for the *New York Times* city beat, the first black hired on the reporter-trainee program, and was then promoted to the reporting staff. She worked at *Life* magazine for two years and at the *New York Times* for thirteen years. In 1969 she was nominated for the Pulitzer Prize for articles on narcotics, civic issues and welfare conditions, civil rights, the poor, blacks, children, and older citizens.

Campbell currently lives in Greenwich Village with her sons Jonathan and Zachary.

Bibliography:

A Girl Called Bob, & A Horse Named Yoki. Dial, 1982.

Carew, Jan Rynveld
[Jan Alwyn Carew] (1925-)
AUTHOR

Most of this author's works are known for their theme: the search for roots. Carew was born in Agricola, Guyana, and has been a professor and department chairman of African-American studies at Northwestern University. He was a senior lecturer in the Council of Humanities and in the Department of Afro-American Studies at Princeton University. From 1966-1969 he lived in Toronto and edited *Cotopax*, a review of third world literature.

In 1969 he was awarded a fellowship from the Canada Arts Council. Carew was editor of *De Kim* in Amsterdam, the *Kensington Post* in London, and the *African Review* in Ghana. In 1974 he won a certificate of excellence from the American Institute of Graphic Arts for *The Third Gift*. In 1975 he set up the Jan Carew Annual Lectureship at Princeton. The same year he won the Burton Annual Fellowship from Howard University's Graduate School of Education. He lives in the Caribbean.

Bibliography:

Rope the Sun. Third Press, 1973 (o.p.).

The Third Gift illustrated by Leo and Diane Dillon. Little, Brown, 1974.

The Twins of Ilora. Little, Brown, 1977 (o.p.).

Children of the Sun. Little, Brown, 1978.

Carter, Mary Kennedy (1934-)
AUTHOR

Carter was born in Franklin, Ohio, and graduated from Ohio State University. She received a master's degree from Columbia University and also attended London University and Makerere University in Kampala, Uganda. She was an elementary school teacher in the Cleveland public schools, a tutor and supervisor of teachers for the Uganda Ministry of Education, a research assistant at Teachers College at Columbia University, and a teacher of black studies in the Roosevelt, New York school district. Other teaching assignments have included her work as professor at the United States Merchant Marine Academy in 1979; as a school consultant for the Baldwin, New York, schools, and as a curriculum writer in the Rockville Center schools from 1983 to the present.

Carter's memberships include the National Council for Social Studies; the National Education Association; the Baldwin Educational Assembly, where she served as member and board member until 1984; and the Jack and Jill Association of America. She was awarded the Afro-Anglo-American Fellowship in 1963. She is married to Donald Wesley Carter and lives in Freeport, New York.

Bibliography:

Count On Me. American Book Company, 1970.

On to Freedom. Hill and Wang, 1970.

Cartey, Wilfred (1931-)
AUTHOR

Born in Port-of-Spain, Trinidad, Cartey earned his bachelor's degree from the University of the West Indies in Jamaica and his master's in fine arts and doctorate from Columbia University.

He has received a Fulbright Travel Grant, a Bernard Van Ler Foundation Fellowship, and a Columbia University Travel and Research Grant.

Cartey was Distinguished Professor of Black Studies at City College in New York in 1973; Professor of Afro-American Studies at the University of California, Berkeley, in 1974; and Resident Professor at the Extra-Mural Department, University of the West Indies.

He was a consultant in African and Afro-American Studies and held the Distinguished Professorship Martin Luther King Chair at City University of New York.

Bibliography:

The West Indies: Islands in the Sun. Nelson, 1967.

Carty, Leo (1931-)
ILLUSTRATOR

When Carty was eleven years old, he won a scholarship to the Museum of Modern Art School. He subsequently studied at Cooper Union, Pratt Institute, and the School of Visual Arts. He lives in Brooklyn with his wife and two children.

Bibliography:

Where Does the Day Go? by Walter Dean Myers. Parents, 1969.

The House On the Mountain by Eleanor Clymer. Dutton, 1971.

I Love Gram by Ruth A. Sonneborn. Viking, 1971.

Chesnutt, Charles Waddell (1858-1932)
AUTHOR

Charles Waddell Chesnutt was born in Cleveland. His parents were freemen who met on their flight north from North Carolina. Young Chesnutt became proficient in reading German, Latin, and French; law; mathematics; and legal stenography. These studies added to his competency as a teacher.

He was a teacher-administrator, principal of the State Normal School in North Carolina, stenographer, journalist, lawyer, and short story writer for the MacClure syndicate and other periodicals. His first published story appeared in a Fayetteville, North Carolina, newspaper. In 1899 his now-famous *The Conjure Woman* appeared.

In 1928 he received the Spingarn Medal from the NAACP for "his pioneer work as a literary artist depicting the life and struggles of Americans of Negro descent, and for his long and useful career as scholar, worker and freeman."

Bibliography:

Conjure Tales by Charles W. Chesnutt, retold by Ray Anthony Shepard. Dutton, 1973 (o.p.).

Childress, Alice (1920-)
AUTHOR

Childress is an actress and writer who puts her theatrical experiences to good use in her books. Her plays for adults have won considerable acclaim: *Trouble in Mind* was awarded an Obie for the best Off-Broadway production in 1955-1956. She has been an actress and director in New York's American Theatre and is a member of the Harlem Writers Guild and the New Dramatists. Many of her articles have appeared in *Freedomways, The Black World* and *Essence* magazines.

She was born in Charleston and grew up and attended school in Harlem. In 1966 she received a Harvard appointment for independent study at Radcliffe Institute. Her work has involved extensive travel through Europe, the USSR and China. She married film editor Nathan Woodard and makes her home in New York.

Bibliography:

A Hero Ain't Nothin' but a Sandwich. Coward, 1973.

When the Rattle Snake Sounds. Coward, 1975.

Let's Hear It for the Queen. Coward, 1976.

Rainbow Jordan. Coward, 1982.

Clifton, Lucille
[Thelma Sayles] (1936-)
AUTHOR

Clifton was born in Depew, New York, and attended Howard University and Fredonia State Teachers College, where she made friends with a small group of blacks interested in theater. She met Ishmael Reed there; he showed her poems to Langston Hughes who published some in his anthology, *Poetry of the Negro*. She also met her husband, Fred Clifton, another member of the group. He was a writer, artist, and philosophy teacher at the University of Buffalo. They married in 1958 and became the parents of six children.

She received the Discovery Award from the YW-YMHA Poetry Center in New York in 1969. *Some of the Days of Everett Anderson* was her first book of poems for children. She received grants from the National Endowment for the Arts from 1969–1972. She was Poet-in-Residence at Coppin State College in Baltimore, a visiting writer at Columbia University School of the Arts, and Poet Laureate of Maryland from 1979 to 1982. She has moved to California since the recent death of her husband.

Bibliography:

The Black BC's illustrated by Don Miller. Dutton, 1970 (o.p.).

All Us Come Cross the Water, illustrated by John Steptoe. Holt, 1973.

The Boy Who Didn't Believe in Spring, illustrated by Brinton Turkle. Dutton, 1973.

The Times They Used To Be, illustrated by Susan Jeschke. Holt, 1974.

The Lucky Stone, illustrated by Dale Payson. Delacorte, 1979.

Everett Anderson's Goodbye, illustrated by Ann Grifalconi. Holt, 1983.

Cornish, Sam (1935-)
AUTHOR

The author grew up in Baltimore and attended Douglass High School, which he left after his first semester. He was in the Medical Corps of the United States Army from 1958-1960 and later attended Goddard College in Vermont. Cornish worked in various places, from an insurance company to bookstores, and later became a consultant on children's writing for the Educational Development Center, Newton, Massachusetts, in their Open Education Follow Through Project.

Bibliography:

Your Hand in Mine. Harcourt, 1970.

Grandmother's Pictures illustrated by Jeanne Johns. Bradbury, 1976.

Crews, Donald (1938–)
ILLUSTRATOR

Crews was born in Newark and attended Arts High School, where admission for music and art training is by competitive examination. He also attended Cooper Union. He served two years of military service in Germany where he married Ann Jonas, a fellow student from Cooper Union. They have two daughters.

Freight Train (1979) and *Truck* (1981) were Caldecott Honor books. *Freight Train* was also an American Library Association Notable Book and a Junior Literary Guild choice along with *Truck* and *Carousel*. In 1979 the American Institute of Graphic Arts Children's Book Show exhibited *Rain* and *Freight Train*. The artist's work has also appeared in *Graphis* magazine.

Bibliography:

Freight Train. Greenwillow, 1978.

Truck. Greenwillow, 1980.

Light. Greenwillow, 1981.

Carousel. Greenwillow, 1982.

Harbor. Greenwillow, 1982.

Parade. Greenwillow, 1983.

School Bus. Greenwillow, 1984.

We Read: A to Z. Greenwillow, 1984.

Bicycle Race. Greenwillow, 1985.

Crichlow, Ernest (1914-)
ILLUSTRATOR

The artist remembers loving to draw since grade school days, when he drew from models suggested by his teacher. After his graduation from Haaren High School in New York, some of his art teachers arranged for his scholarship at Commercial Illustration School of Art and raised money for his art supplies.

His collaboration with Lorraine and Jerrold Beim on *Two Is a Team*, an easy book about the interracial friendship of two little boys, was the beginning of a successful career in children's book illustration, generally on black themes. His art work has been exhibited in many art shows. He has taught at Shaw University, State University of New York at New Paltz, City College of New York, and the Brooklyn Museum Art School.

With N. Lewis and Romare H. Bearden he founded the Cinque Gallery, and co-directs a group of black artists at Saratoga, under the aegis of the State Education Department of Arts and Humanities. Crichlow is also a member of the Black Academy of Arts and Letters.

Crichlow is married and has one son. He and his family live in Brooklyn.

Bibliography:

Two Is a Team by Lorraine and Jerrold Beim. Harcourt, 1945.

Mary Jane by Dorothy Sterling. Scholastic, 1959 (o.p.).

Forever Free by Dorothy Sterling. Doubleday, 1963 (o.p.).

Freedom Train: The Story of Harriet Tubman by Dorothy Sterling. Doubleday, 1963 (o.p.).

Lift Every Voice by Dorothy Sterling and Benjamin Quarles. Doubleday, 1964 (o.p.).

The Magic Mirrors by Judith Griffin. Coward, 1971 (o.p.).

Cullen, Countee [Porter] (1903-1946)
AUTHOR

The scholarly Cullen was among the most respected poets to emerge from the Harlem Renaissance of the 1920s-1930s. He was adopted by Rev. and Mrs. Frederick A. Cullen. Young Countee was an outstanding student at De Witt Clinton High School, at the time was one of the best in New York. He was vice-president of his graduating senior class, editor of the *Clinton News*, and chairman and editor of the senior edition of the school's literary magazine, *The Magpie*. He was also treasurer of an Inter-High School Poetry Society. Cullen was a member of the school's honor society and Arista, and graduated with honors in at least five subjects: Latin, English, French, history and mathematics.

Cullen began writing poetry as a child. In high school he won a second prize for the poem "In Memory of Lincoln" and a contest prize for his well-known "I Have a Rendezvous With Life." He attended New York University, was elected to Phi Beta Kappa—one of a few to receive the honor in 1925 from that college—and in the same year won the Witter Bynner undergraduate poetry contest and second prize in the *Opportunity* literary contest—second only to Langston Hughes.

His first collection of poems, *Color*, published by Harper & Brothers, won the Harmon Foundation's award for literature, awarded by the NAACP for "distinguished achievement in literature by a Negro." He received his master's in English from Harvard University in 1926 and was assistant editor of *Opportunity, A Journal of Negro Life*, in which his monthly column, "The Dark Tower," appeared.

Bibliography:
The Lost Zoo. Follett, 1940.

Cummings, Pat Marie (1950-)
ILLUSTRATOR

Pat Cummings was born in Chicago; as part of an army family Cummings spent her childhood in many places in and out of the United States. She received her bachelor's degree from Pratt Institute in 1974.

In 1974 she became a free-lance illustrator and is currently a professor of design at Queensborough Community College. She is a board member of the Black Art Directors' group in New York and a member of the Graphic Artist Guild.

In 1984 the illustrations for *My Mama Needs Me* won the Coretta Scott King Award and in 1983 her illustrations for *Just Us Women* merited an honorable mention. She also received the CEBA award for an illustration advertising Con Edison, and an honorable mention in 1978 for a poster for the United Nations Committee on Apartheid.

Cummings is married to Chucku Emeka Lee. They live in Brooklyn.

Bibliography:

Good News by Eloise Greenfield. Coward, 1977.

Just Us Women by Jeannette Caines. Harper, 1982.

My Mama Needs Me by Mildred Pitts Walter. Lothrop, 1983.

Chilly Stomach, by Jeannette Caines. Harper, 1986.

C.L.O.U.D.S. Lothrop, 1986.

Springtime Bears by Cathy Warren. Lothrop, 1987.

Davis, Ossie (1917-)
AUTHOR

Davis is an actor, playwright and director born in Cogdell, Georgia. He has held a variety of jobs; he served as a surgical technician in the United States Army's Special Services during World War II, 1942-1945. He has acted on stage, screen, and television, where he and his actress wife, are currently appearing on Howard University's WBBM-TV's third season of "In Other Words . . . *Ossie and Ruby*." He recently completed a production of *Bingo* at an AMAS Repertory Theatre.

His children's books are plays based on major figures in black history: Frederick Douglass and Langston Hughes. Davis is married to Ruby Ann Wallace (Ruby Dee) and has three children: Nora, Guy, and LaVerne. They live in New Rochelle.

Bibliography:

Escape to Freedom: A Play About Young Frederick Douglass. Viking, 1978.

Langston, A Play. Delacorte, 1982.

Deveaux, Alexis (1948-)
AUTHOR

Deveaux, recognized as a poet, novelist, and playwright, was born and raised in New York. Her many theater workshops, appearances on radio and television talk shows, and poetry readings have popularized her work. She taught creative writing, and wrote a novel, *Spirits in the Street*, and a biographical prose poem, "Don't Explain: A Song for Billie Holiday." She worked for the Urban League, taught for the Neighborhood Youth Corps, and was the poetry editor of *Essence* magazine. Her plays—*Circles, Tapestry,* and *A Season to Unravel,* which was performed by the Negro Ensemble Company in New York in 1979—display her interest in the theater.

Bibliography:

na-ni written and illustrated by Alexis Deveaux. Harper, 1973.

Don't Explain: A Song for Billie Holiday. Harper, 1980.

An Enchanted Hair Tale illustrated by Cheryl Hanna. Harper, 1987.

Dillon, Leo (1933-)
ILLUSTRATOR

Born in Brooklyn, Dillon attended AIGA Workshop, Parsons School of Design, and the School of Visual Arts. He and his wife Diane work as a team; they met at Parsons and married shortly after graduation. They have illustrated book jackets, magazines such as *The Ladies Home Journal*, posters, and children's books.

Their books have won many honors and awards. *Song of the Boat* won the Boston and Globe Horn Book Honor Award for illustrations. Their Caldecott-winning books: *Why Mosquitoes Buzz in People's Ears* and *Ashanti to Zulu: African Traditions*, are only two of the widely-acclaimed books they have embellished.

Leo and Diane Dillon have one son, Lee, and live in Brooklyn.

Bibliography:

Behind the Back of the Mountain: Black Folktales from Southern Africa retold by Verna Aardema, illustrated by Leo and Diane Dillon. Dial, 1973.

Songs and Stories from Uganda by W. Moses Serwadda, illustrated by Leo and Diane Dillon. Crowell, 1974.

The Third Gift by Jan Carew. Little, Brown, 1974.

Why Mosquitoes Buzz in People's Ears retold by Verna Aardema, illustrated by Leo and Diane Dillon. Dial, 1975.

The Hundred Penny Box by Sharon Bell Mathis, illustrated by Leo and Diane Dillon. Viking, 1975.

Ashanti to Zulu: African Traditions by Margaret Musgrove, illustrated by Leo and Diane Dillon. Dial, 1976.

Honey I Love by Eloise Greenfield, illustrated by Leo and Diane Dillon. Crowell, 1978.

The People Could Fly by Virginia Hamilton, illustrated by Leo and Diane Dillon. Knopf, 1985.

Mother Crocodile = Maman-Caiman by Birago Diop, translated by Rosa Guy, illustrated by Leo and Diane Dillon. Delacorte, 1981.

Listen Children: Anthology of Black Literature edited by Dorothy Strickland, illustrated by Leo and Diane Dillon. Bantam, 1982.

Diop, Birago (1906-)
AUTHOR

This son of a Wolof father was born in Ouakam, a suburb of Dakar, Senegal. He went to school in Rue Thiong, Dakar, and later won a scholarship to Lycee Faidherbe in Saint-Louis, Senegal. He worked as a nurse in a military hospital in Saint-Louis, and obtained a scholarship to study veterinary medicine. He left Senegal to study at the University of Toulouse in France, where he received his degree as a veterinary surgeon. While studying in Paris he met Leopold Senghor, the first president of Senegal and noted African poet. Diop was later appointed ambassador of Senegal to Tunisia.

His tales of Amadou Koumba as told by the griots, traditional West African storytellers, are described by Senghor: "restores the fables and ancient Tales, in their spirit and in their style."

Bibliography:

Jojo. Third Press, 1970.

Tales of Amadou Koumba, translated by Rosa Guy as *Mother Crocodile.* Delacorte, 1981.

Dunbar, Paul Laurence (1872-1906)
AUTHOR

"Little brown baby wif' spa'klin' eyes,
Who's pappy's darlin' an' who is pappy's chile? . . ."
Although he preferred writing in standard English, Dunbar was best-known for his poetry in dialect. Paul Dunbar was born in Dayton on June 27, 1872. His widowed mother, an ex-slave, married Joshua Dunbar who died when Paul was twelve years old. His mother could read and write and encouraged young Paul with his writing. He attended Dayton public schools. At Central High School he had great success with his peers and teachers. He was member of the school's literary society and wrote for the school paper, editing the paper in his senior year. Dunbar worked as an elevator operator and courthouse messenger, and while working at the Chicago World's Fair in 1893, he met Frederick Douglass, then commissioner of the Haitian exhibit, who hired him as a clerical assistant.

With the help of many white friends and the introduction written by leading literary critic William Dean Howells to his third collection of poems *Lyrics of Lowly Life*, Dunbar achieved wide recognition. Tuskegee's school song was among his many works. In spite of his personal evaluation of his work, his dialect poetry is considered his best.

The poet married schoolteacher Alice Ruth Moore, in 1898. From then until his death at the age of thirty-four he was active in social and educational circles.

Bibliography:

Complete Poems of Paul Lawrence Dunbar. Dodd, 1938.
Little Brown Baby. Dodd, 1940.

Edwards, Audrey (1947-)
AUTHOR

Born in Tacoma, Washington, Edwards earned her bachelor's degree at the University of Washington and her master's degree from Columbia University. She was a free-lance writer, contributing articles to the *Daily News* and the *New York Times*, and *Black Enterprise* and *Redbook* magazines. She was a senior editor of *Family Circle* magazine, a reporter for Fairchild Publications, and City Editor of *Community News Service*, a black and Puerto Rican news service. She also taught at New York University and the New School for Social Research.

Among her awards is the Coretta Scott King Fellowship from the American Association of University Women in 1969. She has been the editor of *Essence* magazine for more than thirteen years.

Bibliography:

The Picture Life of Bobby Orr with Gary Wohl. Watts, 1976.

The Picture Life of Muhammad Ali with Gary Wohl. Watts, 1976.

Muhammad Ali, the People's Champ with Gary Wohl. Watts, 1977.

The Picture Life of Stevie Wonder with Gary Wohl. Watts, 1977.

Egypt, Ophelia Settle (1903-1984)
AUTHOR

Egypt was born in Clarksville, Texas. She worked as an educator, social service administrator, and writer, and will be remembered for her work as director of a home for black unwed mothers and as founder in 1981 of one of Washington, D.C.'s first birth counseling clinics, the Parklands Egypt Clinic, which has served over 1,800 clients.

Educated at Howard University, the University of Pennsylvania, and Columbia University, she was consultant to governmental and social service organizations and a member of many associations in the social service field. She was an instructor at Fisk University, and Assistant Professor and field work supervisor at Howard University medical school.

Her *Unwritten History of Slavery* was a collection of interviews conducted with former slaves during her travels in Kentucky and Tennessee from 1929-1931. She received the Iota Phi Lambda Sorority's Woman of the Year Award in 1963, the International Women's Year Award, and the Club Twenty Award in 1975. At the time of her death in Washington, D.C. she was preparing a children's edition of her slave interviews.

Bibliography:
James Weldon Johnson. Crowell, 1974.

Emecheta, Buchi
[Florence Onye] (1944-)
AUTHOR

The author was born in Lagos, Nigeria. Her father, a railroad porter, died when she was still quite young. Emecheta displayed advanced intellectual ability at an early age and attended Methodist Girls' High School from age ten. After winning a scholarship she followed her husband to London; they later separated and Emecheta was left with the support of their five children. She eventually earned an honor's degree in sociology from London University. Her persistence in writing and submitting manuscripts resulted in the publication of a number of her articles in the *New Statesman*. Since 1962 she has lived in London, where she works as a sociologist and writer of historical novels.

Bibliography:

Nowhere to Play illustrated by Peter Araber. Schocken, 1981.

The Moonlight Bride. Braziller, 1983.

The Wrestling Match. Braziller, 1983.

Evans, Mari (1926-)
AUTHOR

Evans was born in Toledo and attended the University of Toledo. She later moved to Indianapolis. Evans, well-known for her talent as a musician, educator, and writer, was an associate professor in the Africana Studies and Research Center at Cornell University, and Writer-in-Residence at many other colleges and universities in addition to her work as an ethnic studies consultant for a publishing firm. She was a television writer and directed "The Black Experience" program. In addition to her political writings she has written three volumes of poetry and four children's books.

She is currently Visiting Associate Professor in the Department of African/Afro-American Studies, State University of New York at Albany. Evans has taught Afro-American literature at Indiana, Northwestern, and Purdue Universities and received the Black Academy of Arts and Letters First Annual Poetry Award.

Bibliography:

J.D. Doubleday, 1973.

I Look at Me. Third World, 1974.

Rap Stories. Third World, 1974.

Jim Flying High. Doubleday, 1979.

Fauset, Jessie [Redmon] (1884?-1961)
AUTHOR

Fauset, the daughter of a minister, was born in Snow Hill, New Jersey. A writer of poetry, short stories, novels, and essays, she is best remembered as the first black female to graduate from Cornell University, a French teacher and the literary editor of *Crisis*.

She published some works of the Harlem Renaissance literary greats, notably, Langston Hughes, when she served as editor of *Crisis* and editor and primary writer for the *Brownies Book*, a magazine for black children published by the NAACP. She died in Philadelphia on April 30, 1961.

Bibliography:

The Brownies Book edited by Jessie Fauset. Dubois and Dill Publishers, 1920-1921.

Fax, Elton (1909-)
AUTHOR/ILLUSTRATOR

The artist was born in Baltimore and received his bachelor's degree from Syracuse University in 1931. Through the years he has given "Chalk Talks" lectures to groups in high schools and elsewhere. He has also worked as a United States Department of State Specialist in South America and the Caribbean, and in East Africa he represented the American Society of African Culture on tour in Nigeria in 1963. He has participated in international educational exchanges.

Fax has held memberships in the American Society of African Culture and the International Platform Association. He won the Coretta Scott King Award in 1972 for *Seventeen Black Artists.*

Bibliography:

West African Vignettes. Dodd, 1963 (o.p.).

Contemporary Black Leaders. Dodd, 1970 (o.p.).

Seventeen Black Artists. Dodd, 1971.

Garvey: Story of a Pioneer Black Nationalist. Dodd, 1972.

Feelings, Muriel [Gray] (1938-)
AUTHOR

Feelings, born in Philadelphia, entered Philadelphia College of Art for one year on a partial scholarship. In 1963 she graduated from California State University at Los Angeles and worked as a teacher in New York, where she met Africans. In 1966 the Uganda Mission to the United Nations recruited her to work as an art teacher in a Kampala high school. Her students' work was considered the basis for publishing literature by the Ministry of Education.

She married Tom Feelings, who had corresponded with her asking for Kampala folk literature. However, because she believes factual information on Africa is needed, her first story was *Zamani Goes to Market*.

In teaching school in Brooklyn, she introduced African crafts and Swahili; the experience culminated in *Moja Means One: Swahili Counting Book*. In 1971 the Feelingses went to work in Guyana. Muriel Feelings taught art in two high schools there; in her second she assisted in editing booklets for school use. Upon her return to the United States she completed *Jambo Means Hello: Swahili Alphabet Book*. Both books have been widely honored, including winning the Caldecott Honor Book Award. Muriel Feelings has lived in Philadelphia since, working for Afro-American concerns. She is currently working in a Philadelphia museum.

Bibliography:

Zamani Goes to Market. Seabury, 1970 (o.p.).

Moja Means One: Swahili Counting Book illustrated by Tom Feelings. Dial, 1971.

Jambo Means Hello: Swahili Alphabet Book illustrated by Tom Feelings. Dial, 1974.

Feelings, Thomas (1933-)

ILLUSTRATOR

Tom Feelings, born and raised in Brooklyn, received a three-year scholarship to Cartoonists and Illustrators School after high school. After four years in the United States Air Force (1953–1959) he attended the School of Visual Arts. His comic strip, *Tommy Traveler in the World of Negro History*, was a feature of Harlem's newspaper *New York Age*.

In 1964 he worked in Ghana for the Ghana Government Publishing Company. He returned to the United States two years later, starting children's books on African and Afro-American subjects. In his work for the Guyana government from 1971–1974, he served as a consultant for the Guyanese Children's Book Division and taught Guyanese illustrators.

He illustrated *Moja Means One* and *Jambo Means Hello*, Caldecott Honor books written by his former wife, Muriel. The illustrations for *Something on My Mind*, words by Nikki Grimes, won the 1979 Coretta Scott King Award. *Daydreamers* by Eloise Greenfield was cited as an honorable mention in 1982.

Bibliography:

To Be a Slave by Julius Lester. Dial, 1968.

Moja Means One by Muriel Feelings. Dial, 1971.

Black Pilgrimage. Lothrop, 1972.

Jambo Means Hello by Muriel Feelings. Dial, 1974.

Something on My Mind by Nikki Grimes. Dial, 1978.

Daydreamers by Tom Feelings and Eloise Greenfield. Dial, 1981.

Joyce Arkhurst.

Lerone Bennett, Jr.

Augusta Baker.

Ashley Bryan.
Photograph by
Sally Stone Halvorson.

Jeannette Caines.
Photograph by Al Cetta.

Mary Kennedy Carter.

Pat Cummings.

Alexis Deveaux.

Donald Crews.
Photograph by
Chuck Kelton.

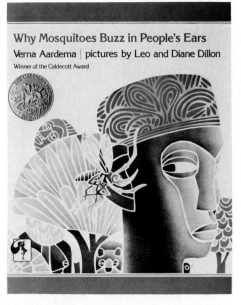

Dust jacket for *Why Mosquitoes Buzz in People's Ears*
by Verna Aardema.

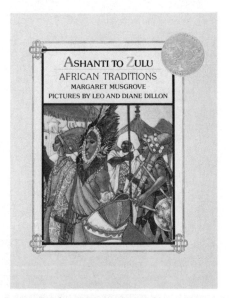

Dust jacket for *Ashanti to Zulu: African Traditions*
by Margaret Musgrove. Pictures by Leo and Diane Dillon.
Courtesy E.P. Dutton

Audrey Edwards.
From a photograph by Risasi-Zachariah Dais.

Elton Fax.

Valerie Flournoy.

Jerry Pinkney.

Julius Lester.
Photograph courtesy Scholastic, Inc.

Dust jacket for *The Patchwork Quilt* by Valerie Flournoy.
Pictures by Jerry Pinkney. Courtesy E.P. Dutton.

Dust jacket for *The Tales of Uncle Remus:*
The Adventures of Brer Rabbit as told by Julius Lester.
Illustrated by Jerry Pinkney. Courtesy E.P. Dutton.

George Ford.

Eloise Greenfield.
Photograph by Tony Hawkins.

Rosa Guy.

Flournoy, Valerie R. (1952-)
AUTHOR

Flournoy is the daughter of Payton I. Flournoy, Sr., retired Palmyra, New Jersey, Chief of Police. She is a twin and the third of five children. Her twin sister Vanessa is author of *All-American Girl*, a Silhouette First Love published in 1983 under the name Vanessa Payton. Her two brothers are both law enforcement officers.

She received her bachelor's degree and teacher's certification in social studies (grades 7–12) from Hobart and William Smith College in Geneva, New York. Her writing interest grew from her publishing experience as a clerk-typist in the School and Library Services division of the Dell Publishing Company. She later became Senior Editor for Silhouette Romance Books/Pocket Books and editorial consultant for another romance line. Her *Patchwork Quilt* received a Christopher Award, the Ezra Jack Keats, and New Writer Award. The illustrations by Jerry Pinkney won the 1986 Coretta Scott King Award.

Flournoy resides in Palmyra.

Bibliography:
The Best Time of Day. Random House, 1978.
The Twins Strike Back. Dial, 1980.
The Patchwork Quilt. Dial, 1985.

Ford, George, Jr. (1936-)
ILLUSTRATOR

The artist was born in Brooklyn and spent part of his childhood in Barbados. His early memories include those of a grandmother who constantly drew portraits on slate with chalk. He credits her with inspiring him to become an artist.

He studied at the Art Students League, Pratt Institute, Cooper Union, the School of Visual Arts, and City College in New York. His art has appeared in *Harper's* magazine and the Brooklyn Museum, including the 1971 exhibition, "Black Artist in Graphic Communications." Ford was Art Director at Eden Advertising and Design Director of *Black Theater* magazine. He illustrated *Ray Charles*, written by Sharon Bell Mathis and winner of the Coretta Scott King Award in 1974.

He is married with one daughter.

Bibliography:

The Singing Turtle and Other Tales from Haiti by Phillipe Thoby-Marcelin. Farrar, 1971.

Walk On by Mel Williamson and George Ford, Jr., illustrated by George Ford, Jr. Third Press, 1972.

Ray Charles by Sharon Bell Mathis. Crowell, 1973.

Ego Tripping and Other Poems for Young People by Nikki Giovanni. Lawrence Hill, 1974.

Paul Robson by Eloise Greenfield. Crowell, 1975.

Far Eastern Beginnings by Olivia Vlahos. Viking, 1976.

Muhammad Ali by Kenneth Rudeen. Crowell, 1976.

Fufuka, Karama
[Sharon Antonia Morgan] (1951-)
AUTHOR

Born in Chicago, the author attended Loop City College, one of the Chicago City Colleges. She has a variety of interests and work experiences as secretary, receptionist, and Associate Director of Provident Community Development Corporation. She has contributed articles to *Ebony Jr.*, *Essence*, and *Lifestyles*, and has been an editor of the *Woodburn Community Observer* since 1975.

Bibliography:

My Daddy Is a Cool Dude and Other Poems illustrated by Mahiri Fufuka. Dial, 1975.

Gayle, Addison (1932-)
AUTHOR

The author, born in Newport News, received his bachelor's degree from City College in New York and his master's degree from the University of California in Los Angeles. A teacher of writing and literature, Gayle was a professor of American and Afro-American literature at the University of Washington and has lectured at City College, serving on the chancellor's committee on prisons and the graduate center's committee on English programs. He was a consultant to minority writers at Doubleday and Random House publishers and has been on the editorial staffs of *Amistad* magazine, *Third World Press*, and *Black Lines* magazine. Donor of the Richard Wright-Amiri Baraka Award for the best critical essay published in *Black World* magazine, he also sponsored the Richard Wright Award for the minority scholarship program, SEEK, given each semester to the student with the highest scholastic average. A member of P.E.N. International and the Authors Guild, Gayle is currently Distinguished Professor of English at Bernard Baruch College in New York.

Bibliography:

Oak and Ivy: A Biography of Paul Laurence Dunbar. Doubleday, 1981.

Giovanni, Nikki [Yolanda C.] (1943-)
AUTHOR

Giovanni earned her bachelor's degree in history at Fisk University, later attending the University of Pennsylvania School of Social Work and Columbia University. Among her awards are a Ford Foundation Grant in 1968 and a National Endowment for the Arts Grant in 1969. Honorary doctorates from Wilberforce University, Smith College, and the University of Maryland, and a citation from *Ebony* in 1969 as one of the ten most admired black women have made her much in demand on the lecture circuit.

Giovanni was Assistant Professor of Black Studies at Queens College of the City University of New York, Associate Professor of English at Livingston College, Rutgers University, and an editorial consultant for *Encore* magazine. She has one son and resides in New York City.

Bibliography:

Spin a Soft Black Song: Poems for Children. Hill and Wang, 1971.

Ego Tripping and Other Poems for Young Readers. Lawrence Hill, 1973.

Vacation Time Poems for Children. Morrow, 1981.

Graham, Lorenz [Bell] (1902-)
AUTHOR

Graham was born in New Orleans and educated at the University of California in Los Angeles. He also attended Virginia Union, New York School of Social Work, and New York University. He taught at Monrovia College, Liberia, from 1925–1929; he has been a probation officer, social worker, and camp adviser for the Civilian Conservation Corps, Virginia from 1934–1945 as well as a writer. His memberships include Kappa Alpha Psi, Southern California Writers' Guild, Authors' League of America, and P.E.N. International. Among his awards are the Thomas Alva Edison Foundation Citation, 1956; the Charles W. Follett Award, 1958; the Child Study Association of America Award, 1958; the Southern California Council of Literature for Children and Young People Award, 1968; and first prize, from Book World, 1969.

Graham lives in California. He married Ruth Morris and has four children.

Bibliography:

North Town. Crowell, 1965.

God Wash the World and Start Again. Crowell, 1971 (o.p.).

Song of the Boat. Crowell, 1975.

Return to South Town. Crowell, 1976 (o.p.).

John Brown: A Cry for Freedom. Crowell, 1980.

Graham, Shirley Lola
[Mrs. W.E.B. DuBois] (1906-1977)
AUTHOR

Graham was born in Indianapolis. She studied music in Paris, obtained a French Certificate from the Sorbonne, and earned her bachelor's and master's degrees from Oberlin College. She also studied at Yale University Drama School and received an Honorory Doctor of Letters from the University of Massachusetts in 1973.

Her work experience includes her position as head of the fine arts department of Tennessee State College, director of the Chicago Federal Theater, YWCA director, field secretary for the NAACP, director of Ghana Television, founding editor of *Freedomways* magazine, and English editor in 1968 of the Afro-Asian Writers Bureau in Peking. She received many awards: a Rosenwald and Guggenheim Fellowship from Yale University Drama School for historical research, and in 1950 the Julian Messner Award for *There Was Once a Slave*.

She married twice and had one son from her first marriage. W.E.B. DuBois was her second husband. She died in Peking on March 27 at age sixty-nine.

Bibliography:

Booker T. Washington: Educator of Hand, Head and Heart. Messner, 1955 (o.p.).

Paul Robeson: Citizen of the World. Messner, 1971 (o.p.).

Julius K. Nyerere: Teacher of Africa. Messner, 1975.

Greenfield, Eloise
[Glynn Little] (1929-)
AUTHOR

"I hope that I can contribute a little in moving children toward their best selves."

Greenfield was born in Parmele, North Carolina, to Weston Wilbur Little and Lessie Blanche [Jones] Little. She has had a number of secretarial positions, and has worked as an administrative assistant in the Department of Occupations and Professions. Her memberships include the adult fiction and children's literature divisions of the D.C. Black Writers Workshop and the Authors Guild. She was Writer-in-Residence at the D.C. Commission on the Arts and Humanities in 1973. She was a lecturer and workshop leader in children's literature, and has received several awards and citations for her books.

In 1974, *Rosa Parks* was cited by the National Council for Social Studies, *She Come Bringing Me That Little Baby Girl* won the Irma Simonton Black Award and was also an American Library Association Notable Book. In 1976 *Paul Robeson* won the Jane Addams Award and *Africa Dream* won the 1978 Coretta Scott King Award. In 1983 she received the Mayor's Art Award in Literature in Washington, D.C. Her grants have come from the D.C. Commission on the Arts and Humanities. Greenfield, formerly married to Robert J. Greenfield, has two children: Steven R. and Monica Joyce.

Bibliography:

Rosa Parks. Crowell, 1973.

She Come Bringing Me That Little Baby Girl. Lippincott, 1974.

Paul Robeson. Crowell, 1975.

Africa Dream. John Day, 1977.

Mary McCleod Bethune. Crowell, 1977.

Honey, I Love. Crowell, 1978.

Little. Crowell, 1979.

Childtimes: A Three-Generation Memoir with Lessie Jones Little. Crowell, 1979.

Grandmama's Joy. Philomel, 1980.

Alesia with Alesia Revis. Philomel, 1981.

Daydreamers. Dial, 1981.

Griffin, Judith Berry
AUTHOR

Griffin obtained both her bachelor's and master's degrees in psychology from the University of Chicago. She later received a master's in special education from Teachers College at Columbia University. She was an elementary school principal in Hartsdale, New York, and has taught elementary school in White Plains, New York, where she lives with her son.

Bibliography:

Nat Turner. Coward, 1970.

The Magic Mirrors. Coward, 1971.

Phoebe and the General illustrated by Margot Tomes. Coward, 1971.

Grimes, Nikki (1950-)
AUTHOR

Grimes majored in English and studied African languages at Livingston College, Rutgers University. She received a Ford Foundation Grant in 1974 that enabled her to spend a year in Tanzania collecting folktales and poetry. Journalism, photography and poetry writing have kept her busy since 1975. Her poetry often appears in anthologies of modern American poetry. She lives in New York City.

Bibliography:

Growin' illustrated by Charles Lilly. Dial, 1977.

Something on My Mind illustrated by Tom Feelings. Dial, 1978.

Guirma, Frederic
AUTHOR/ILLUSTRATOR

Guirma was born in Ouagadougou, Upper Volta. He claims Naba Koumdoum 'ue', the eighth emperor of the Mois people in the fourteenth century, to be one of his ancestors. Guirma attended an elementary school taught by the Sisters of Our Lady of Africa and later the Seminary of Padre. He received his bachelor's degree in France and a master's degree from Loyola University in Los Angeles.

He has been Secretary of the French Embassy in Ghana and served as Vice-Counsul in Kumesi, Ghana. When Upper Volta became an independent nation in 1960, he was its first ambassador to the United Nations and Washington, D.C. He has also been Senior Political Affairs Officer at United Nations headquarters.

In his spare time Guirma writes and paints. His book *Princess of the Full Moon*, which he wrote and illustrated, is based on folklore of Upper Volta.

Bibliography:

Princess of the Full Moon. Macmillan, 1970.

Tales of Mogho: African Stories from Upper Volta. Macmillan, 1971.

Guy, Rosa [Cuthbert] (1928-)
AUTHOR

Rosa Guy was born in Trinidad, the daughter of Henry and Audrey [Gonzales] Cuthbert. She was brought to the United States in 1932, grew up in Harlem, and later attended New York University.

Guy is a founder and former president of the Harlem Writers Guild. She has traveled to Africa, Senegal, Mali, Gambia, Algeria, Nigeria, Haiti, and to her birthplace. She speaks French and Creole, and researches African articles.

Her magazine articles have appeared in *Cosmopolitan* and *Freedomways*. *The Friends*, first of a trilogy of novels for young people, was cited as among the "Best Books for Young Adults" by the American Library Association and selected as the *New York Times* Outstanding Book of the Year in 1976. Other books in the trilogy are *Ruby* and *Edith Jackson*. Guy's book for younger children, *Mother Crocodile*, illustrated by John Steptoe, was an American Library Association Notable Book and won the 1982 Coretta Scott King Award. Guy is the widow of Warner Guy. She has one son, Warner.

Bibliography:

The Friends. Holt, 1973.

Ruby. Viking, 1976.

Edith Jackson. Viking, 1978.

Mother Crocodile = Maiman-Caiman illustrated by John Steptoe. Delacorte, 1981.

New Guys Around the Block. Viking, 1983.

And I Heard a Bird Sing. Delacorte, 1987.

Hamilton, Virginia Esther (1933-)
AUTHOR

Hamilton was born in southern Ohio, where her maternal ancestors settled after the Civil War.

John Rowe Townsend, in *Written for Children*, describes Virginia Hamilton as "the most subtle and interesting of today's black writers for children." Hamilton's books have always centered around black heritage and more personally around her own family history. Her themes go beyond family experiences, weaving mysticism, fantasy, and realism.

Hamilton has received many major literary awards and much recognition for her children's books. *M.C. Higgins the Great* won the 1975 Newbery Medal, the National Book Award, and the Boston-Globe-Horn Book Award. *The Planet of Junior Brown* and *Sweet Whispers, Brother Rush* were Newbery Honor Books. She was also awarded two Certificates of Honor by the International Board of Books for Young People (IBBY) for these books. The awards cited the books as outstanding examples of literature with international importance. Hamilton won the Coretta Scott King Award in 1983 and 1986. "The Virginia Hamilton Lectureship on Minority Experiences in Children's Literature" at Kent State University was established in her honor.

Hamilton credits her parents Kenneth and Etta Belle Perry Hamilton for her storytelling ability. She now resides in Yellow Springs, Ohio, with her husband, poet Arnold Adoff and their two children. Hamilton and Adoff are writers-in-residence at Queens College of the City University of New York for 1987 and 1988.

Bibliography:

Zeely. Macmillan, 1967.
The House of Dies Drear. Collier, 1968.

The Time-Ago Tales of Jadhu. Macmillan, 1968.

The Planet of Junior Brown. Macmillan, 1971.

M.C. Higgins, the Great. Macmillan, 1974.

Paul Robeson: The Life and Times of a Free Black Man. Harper, 1974.

The Writings of W.E.B. Du Bois edited by Virginia Hamilton. Crowell, 1975.

Sweet Whispers, Brother Rush. Philomel, 1982.

The Magical Adventures of Pretty Pearl. Harper, 1983.

The People Could Fly. Knopf, 1985.

The Mystery of Drear House. Greenwillow, 1987.

Hansen, Joyce W. (1942-)
AUTHOR

"Some writers have recurring or favorite themes—mine are: the importance of family, belief in self, maintaining a sense of hope and a determination to overcome obstacles and being responsible for oneself and other living things.

"I try to flesh out those things that are intrinsic to the Afro-American experience—those positive aspects of our lives that should not be discarded—our extended families, our concern and respect for the elderly, and our sense of community."

Hansen was born in New York, attended Pace University, and received her master's degree from New York University in 1978. She has worked as an administrative assistant at Pace University, and since 1973 as a teacher of remedial reading and English for the New York City Board of Education. Her novel *The Gift Giver* received the Spirit of Detroit Award and was also designated Notable Children's Trade Book in the field of social studies in 1980. Hansen claims that her stories come from youngsters: "My own stories come as chunks of reality—ideas that are generated by the young people I know and work with."

Bibliography:

The Gift Giver. Houghton, 1980.

Home Boy. Clarion, 1982.

Yellow Bird and Me. Clarion, 1986.

Which Way Freedom? Walker, 1986.

Haskins, James S. (1941-)
AUTHOR

The author was born in Demopolis, Alabama, where he remembers a childhood "in a household with lots of children." He attended high school in Boston and college "in a variety of places. . . . I write books for adults, but most of the books I write are for young people. It is my feeling that adults either read or do not read depending on how they felt about books when they were young . . . my own experience, from childhood on, is that reading books is a nice way to carve out your own private world and learn about the big world at the same time. But you must find out about the wonder of reading when you are young. If you find it out then, it doesn't matter whether you are allowed into the library or not; you will find a way to get books."

Haskins has a bachelor's degree in psychology from Georgetown University and one in history from Alabama State University; he received his master's degree from the University of New Mexico in 1963. He also attended the New York Institute of Finance, earning a certificate of Work of the Stock Exchange; the New School for Social Research; and Queens College of the City University of New York's graduate program in psychology. He has taught in high school and college; he is currently a professor in the English department at the University of Florida in Gainesville.

His memberships include Phi Beta Kappa; the National Advisory Committee, Statue of Liberty—Ellis Island Commission; National Book Critics Circle; 100 Black Men; and the Authors Guild. Many of his books have been selected as Notable Children's Books by *Social Studies* magazine. *Barbara Jordan* was selected by the Child Study Association in 1979, and the *Story of Stevie Wonder* won the Coretta Scott King Award in 1977.

Bibliography:

The Picture Life of Malcom X. Watts, 1975.

The Story of Stevie Wonder. Lothrop, 1976.

Andrew Young: Man with a Mission. Lothrop, 1979.

James Van Der Zee: The Picture Takin' Man. Dodd, 1979.

The New Americans: Vietnamese Boat People. Enslow, 1980.

Black Theater in America. Crowell, 1982.

Space Challenger: The Story of Guion Bluford with Kathleen Benson. Carolrhoda Books, 1984.

Black Music in America: A History Through Its People. Crowell, 1987.

Count Your Way Through China illustrated by Dennis Hockerman, Carolrhoda, 1987.

Count Your Way Through Japan illustrated by Martin Skoro. Carolrhoda, 1987.

Count Your Way Through Russia illustrated by Vera Mednikov. Carolrhoda, 1987.

Count Your Way Through the Arab World illustrated by Dana Gustafson. Carolrhoda, 1987.

Howard, Moses Leon
[Musa Nagenda] (1928-)
AUTHOR

The author, born in Copiah County, Mississippi, received his bachelor's degree at Alcorn A.&M. College and his master's from Case Western Reserve University. He did further graduate study at the University at Alaska, New York University, and Columbia University.

Howard has worked as a steelworker, biology and chemistry instructor, and science department head at National Teachers' College, and served at the African Ministry of Education in Kampala, Uganda. He taught public school in Seattle. Howard was named Outstanding Educator of the Year in Washington state in 1981.

Bibliography:

Dogs of Fear. Holt, 1972. (Published under the name Musa Nagenda.)

The Human Mandolin. Holt, 1974.

The Ostrich Chase. Holt, 1974.

Hughes, Langston [James](1902-1967)
AUTHOR

Dubbed the "Negro Poet Laureate," Hughes, a product of the Harlem Renaissance, was a tremendously prolific writer. He was born in Joplin, Missouri, in 1902, son of James Nathaniel Hughes and Carrie Langston Hughes. He lived with his grandmother in Kansas after his parents' separation. When his mother remarried, young Hughes lived with her and his stepfather in Cleveland.

He started to write poetry in the eighth grade and was elected class poet. After high school graduation Hughes visited his father in Mexico, and to please him attended Columbia University, though he only stayed one year. Then began his travels to Europe and Africa, an opportunity to experience life, observe people, and work at various jobs before returning to the United States.

In 1929 he graduated from Lincoln University. In 1935 he won a Guggenheim Fellowship and in 1941 a Rosenwald Fellowship, the first of a host of honors he was to receive for his writing. Hughes wrote poetry, a play, newspaper articles and columns, a novel, essays, lyrics for a successful musical, and children's books. His poetry is a mix of blank verse, dialect, and lyric verse, reflecting his interest in language, rhythm, and the music he loved—jazz and the blues. His prize works demonstrate his political and social activism and his disapproval of civil injustices against his people, but his work is distinguished by its brilliant humor and witty satire.

In 1946 he was an elected member of the National Institute of Arts and Letters; he was a visiting professor of creative writing at Atlanta University, 1947–1948, and Poet-in-Residence at the Laboratory School, University of Chicago in 1949–1950. His honorary doctorates were awarded by Lincoln University and Case Western Reserve University. His living depended solely on his earnings from writing and lecturing. He made his home in his beloved Harlem.

Bibliography:

The Dream Keeper and Other Poems illustrated by Helen Sewell. Knopf, 1937, 1986 (introduction by Augusta Baker).

Famous American Negroes. Dodd, 1954 (o.p.).

Famous Negro Music Makers. Dodd, 1955 (o.p.).

The First Book of Africa. Watts, 1964 (o.p.).

Black Misery. Erikson, 1969 (o.p.).

Don't You Turn Back selected by Lee Bennett Hopkins. Knopf, 1969.

Jazz (original title, *The First Book of Jazz*). Updated Edition. Watts, 1982.

A Pictorial History of Black Americans. by Langston Hughes, Milton Meltzer, and C. Eric Lincoln. Fifth Revised Ed. Crown, 1984.

Hunter, Kristin (1931-)
AUTHOR

Hunter was born in Philadelphia and attended school there, receiving her bachelor's degree in 1951 in education from the University of Pennsylvania. She has been a teacher, copywriter for Lavenson Bureau of Advertising in Philadelphia, research assistant at the University of Pennsylvania's School of Social Work, and the City of Philadelphia's Information Officer.

Her awards and honors include: Fund for the Republic Prize for a television documentary, the Book World Festival Award, the Council on Interracial Books for Children Award in 1968, the Christopher Award in 1974, a Whitney Fellowship, a Sigma Delta Chi Award for reporting, and a Brotherhood Award from the National Conference of Christians and Jews. She currently lectures in creative writing at the University of Pennsylvania.

Bibliography:

The Soul Brothers and Sister Lou. Scribner's, 1968.

Boss Cat. Scribner's, 1971.

Guests in the Promised Land. Scribner's, 1973.

Lou in the Limelight. Scribner's, 1981.

Jackson, Jesse (1908-1983)
AUTHOR

The author was born in Columbus and attended Ohio State University, where he was active in boxing and track. He entered the Olympic trials and planned to become a professional boxer, but he later changed his mind. His summers were spent at various jobs: boxing in a carnival, working on a steamer on the Great Lakes, and "jerking sodas" in Atlantic City. He worked in boys' camps and with private youth agencies, served as a juvenile probation officer and worked for the Bureau of Economic Research.

His first writing venture was in collaboration with artist Calvin Bailey on a series of articles on boxers. The articles were sold to New York newspapers. He said his first book for children, *Call Me Charlie*, was written as "a small tribute to the good people who somehow or other succeed in making bad things better." In 1974 he became a lecturer at Appalachian State University. Among his awards are a MacDowell Colony Fellowship and the National Council for the Social Studies Carter G. Woodson Award in 1975.

Bibliography:

Call Me Charley illustrated by Doris Spiegel. Harper, 1945.

Anchor Man illustrated by Doris Spiegel. Harper, 1947.

Room for Randy illustrated by Frank Nicholas. Friendship Press, 1957.

Charley Starts from Scratch. Harper, 1958.

Tessie illustrated by Harold James. Harper, 1968.

The Sickest Don't Always Die the Quickest. Doubleday, 1971.

The Fourteenth Cadillac. Doubleday, 1972.

Queen of Gospel Singers. Crowell, 1974.

Make a Joyful Noise unto the Lord: The Life of Mahalia Jackson. Crowell, 1974.

Johnson, James Weldon (1871-1938)
AUTHOR

James Weldon Johnson was born in 1871 in Jacksonville, Florida, where he attended city schools and then attended Atlanta University. He first became an elementary school principal, developing the school's program until it became a high school.

He and his brother J. Rosamond Johnson moved to New York and worked together on writing songs and musicals. During this time James Weldon Johnson attended Columbia University for graduate study in drama and literature. He had already received a law degree and practiced law in Florida.

Johnson is probably best known for the "national Negro anthem," "Lift Every Voice and Sing." He wrote the words and his brother the music. While serving as United States Consul in Venezuela and Nicaragua he wrote *The Autobiography of an Ex-Colored Man*. He contributed articles to magazines, translated the libretto of Spanish opera *Coyescas*, and served for many years as Secretary and Field Secretary of the NAACP. He was awarded the Spingarn Medal in 1925. Johnson died in a tragic accident in 1938.

Bibliography:

God's Trombones illustrated by Aaron Douglas. Viking, 1927.

Along This Way. Viking/Penguin, 1968 (o.p.).

Lift Every Voice and Sing by James Weldon Johnson with J. Rosamond Johnson, illustrated by Mozelle Thompson. Hawthorn, 1970 (o.p.).

Jordan, June (1936-)
AUTHOR

Jordan was born in Harlem, and grew up in the Bedford-Stuyvesant section of Brooklyn. She attended Barnard College and the University of Chicago, and taught English at Connecticut College, City College, City University of New York, Sarah Lawrence College, and the State University of New York at Stony Brook.

Among her awards are a Rockefeller Foundation Fellowship in creative writing, the Rome Prize Fellowship in Environmental Design, 1970–1971, and a C.A.P.S. Grant in poetry. Her publications include essays, poetry, newspaper articles and books for young people. Her work has appeared in the *New York Times*, *Partisan Review*, *Village Voice*, and *The Nation*. She has worked in films, with Mobilization for Youth, and as Co-Director of The Voice of the Children, Inc. and its writers' workshop. *His Own Where* was a National Book Award finalist and an American Library Association Best Book for young adults. She was married and has one son.

Bibliography:

Who Look at Me. Crowell, 1969 (o.p.).

The Voice of the Children collected by June Jordan and Terri Bush. Holt, 1970 (o.p.).

His Own Where. Crowell, 1971.

Fannie Lou Hamer. Crowell, 1972 (o.p.).

New Life: New Room. Crowell, 1975 (o.p.).

Kimako's Story. Houghton, 1981.

Kirkpatrick, Oliver Austin
[John Canoe] (1911-)
AUTHOR

The author is also known by his pseudonym, John Canoe. He was born and educated in Jamaica, and after coming to the United States attended New York University, the New School for Social Research, and Columbia University, where he obtained his master's degree in library science.

Kirkpatrick was a columnist and sports editor for the *Jamaica Standard* and a newscaster on radio Jamaica ZQI before working as a librarian in The New York Public Library and a supervising librarian in The Brooklyn Public Library, from which he retired. He received the Joyce Kilmer Award from New York University for creative writing. He is retired and lives in Brooklyn.

Bibliography:

Naja the Snake and Mangus the Mongoose. Doubleday, 1970.

Lawrence, Jacob (1917-)
ILLUSTRATOR

One of the most outstanding comtemporary painters, Lawrence has been called "the nation's foremost Negro painter." His work has been compared favorably with that of Picasso, Daumier, Orozco, and especially Hogarth.

He was born in Atlantic City, on September 17, 1917, but moved when he was two years old with his parents to Easton, Pennsylvania, where the family was abandoned by his father. His mother later moved the family to Philadelphia and then to New York when Lawrence was twelve.

Lawrence studied at the American Artists School on a full scholarship. His spare time was spent at the 135th Street branch of The New York Public Library and at the Schomburg Collection to gather material for a pictorial biography of Frederick Douglass. In 1940 he received a Rosenwald Fellowship to research Southern migrants in the North after World War I. His Rosenwald Foundation Grant of 1941-1942 enabled him to produce his Life of John Brown with a series of twenty-two paintings. The United States Coast Guard Archives houses his World War II pictures. A Guggenheim Fellowship in 1945 helped him produce in 1947 fourteen paintings of World War II. His 1973 George Washington Bush series bears the caption: "Thank God All-Mighty, home at last!"

His style, described as being a series of large flat forms, with "no depth, and no details," is known for the use of pure colors: blues, reds, yellows. Each picture has a title so that the series in sequence resembles a story's script.

Bibliography:

Harriet and the Promised Land. Simon and Schuster, 1968.

Lester, Julius (1939-)
AUTHOR

The author was born in St. Louis. His family moved to Kansas City and then to Nashville during his early adolescence. Lester earned his bachelor's degree in English at Fisk University. He attributes his interest in Southern rural traditions and black folkfore to his father, a Methodist minister and a good storyteller.

Among his other work experiences, Julius Lester has been a social services investigator, folk singer, guitar teacher, and teacher of black history at the New School for Social Research in 1968-1970. He also hosted a talk show on WBAI-FM radio in New York from 1969-1972. He is a professor of black studies at the University of Massachusetts.

His political activities include experience in the late 1960s as a field secretary and head of the photo department, Student Non-Violent Coordinating Committee. In 1967 he took photographs of North Vietnam to show the effects of United States bombing there, and also attended the Organization of Latin American Solidarity Conference in Cuba with Stokeley Carmichael.

The critical responses from children to his first children's book, *To Be A Slave*, convinced him of the difficulty in writing for these readers. As a father of two children he felt the need to write the sort of books unavailable during his own childhood. Lester has written books for adults and his writings have also appeared in newspapers and journals such as the *Village Voice*, *Ebony*, *New York Free Press*, *New York Times Book Review*, *Broadside* and *Parent's Choice*. He has written poetry and edited poetry anthologies. His interest in music shows in his work with Pete Seeger: *The Twelve-Stringed Guitar as Played by Leadbelly*.

To Be a Slave was a Newbery Honor Book in 1969, and winner of the 1968 Nancy Bloch Award. *Long Journey Home* in 1972 and *Black Folktales* in 1969 were on the *New York Times* list of outstanding books of the year. *Long Journey Home* was nominted for a National Book Award in 1973. Lester lives in Amherst, Massachusetts, with his wife and four children.

Bibliography:

To Be a Slave edited by Julius Lester, illustrated by Tom Feelings. Dial, 1968.

The Knee-High Man and Other Tales illlustrated by Ralph Pinto. Dial, 1972.

Long Journey Home: Stories from Black History. Dial, 1972.

This Strange New Feeling. Dial, 1982.

The Tales of Uncle Remus: The Adventures of Brer Rabbit illustrated by Jerry Pinkney. Dial, 1987.

Lilly, Charles
ILLUSTRATOR

The illustrator of *Philip Hall Likes Me* studied at the School of Visual Arts, where he also taught a painting class. His work has appeared in magazine and book jacket illustrations, and his art has been recognized by awards of merit from the Society of Illustrators, the Art Directors Club, and Publication Designers.

Bibliography:

Mukasa by John Nagenda. Macmillan, 1973.

Growin' by Nikki Grimes. Dial, 1977.

Philip Hall Likes Me. I Reckon Maybe by Bette Greene. Dial, 1977.

Lloyd, Errol (1943-)
AUTHOR/ILLUSTRATOR

Lloyd's interest in art started at about age sixteen, after he had decided on a legal career. Lloyd was born in Jamaica and attended Munro College, Jamaica; London University; and Council of Legal Education in London. In 1964 Lloyd started to study law, but his interest in art outweighed this pursuit. His illustrations for *My Brother Sean* were commended for the Kate Greenaway Medal in England in 1977.

Bibliography:

Shawn Goes to School by Petronella Breinburg. Crowell, 1973 (o.p.).

Shawn's Red Bike by Petronella Breinburg, Crowell, 1976 (o.p.).

Nini at Carnival written and illustrated by Errol Lloyd. Crowell, 1978.

Lynch, Lorenzo (1932-)
ILLUSTRATOR

The artist took a correspondence course from Art Instruction, Inc., Minneapolis, from 1946-1950. He attended the Art Students League and the School of Visual Arts. He worked as an artist with Fisher Advertising in Brooklyn, at Olivetti, New York, Martin's Department Store in Brooklyn, and New York's Annivette Studios. He lives in Brooklyn, New York.

Bibliography:

The Hot Dog Man. Bobbs-Merrill, 1970.

The Black is Beautiful Beauty Book by Melba Miller. Prentice-Hall, 1974.

Big Sister Tells Me That I'm Black by Arnold Adoff. Holt, 1976.

Virginia Hamilton.
Photograph by Cox Studios.

Dust jacket for *M.C. Higgins, the Great* by Virginia Hamilton.
Courtesy Macmillan Children's Book Group.

Tom Feelings.

Dust jacket for *Something on My Mind*.
Illustrated by Tom Feelings. Words by Nikki Grimes.
Courtesy E.P. Dutton.

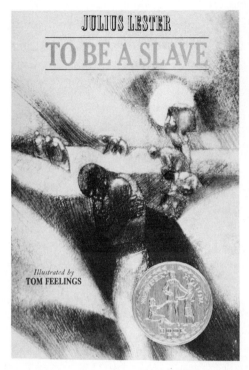

Dust jacket for *To Be a Slave* by Julius Lester.
Illustrated by Tom Feelings. Courtesy E.P. Dutton.

Dust jackets for *Moja Means One: Swahili Counting Book*
and *Jambo Means Hello* by Muriel Feelings.
Pictures by Tom Feelings. Courtesy E.P. Dutton.

Joyce Hansen.
Photograph by Austin Hansen.

Jim Haskins.
Photograph by
George Gray Photography.

June Jordan.

Walter Dean Myers.

Ann Petry.

Reynold Ruffins.

John Steptoe.

Eleanor Tate.
Photograph by Zack Hamlett, III,
Positive Images, Inc.

Ianthe Thomas.
Photograph by Jonny S. Buchsbaum.

Dust jacket for *Philip Hall Likes Me. I Reckon Maybe*
by Bette Greene. Pictures by Charles Lilly. Courtesy E.P. Dutton.

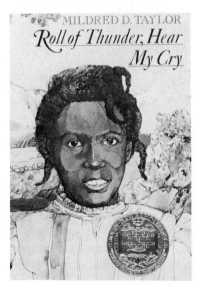

Dust jacket for *Roll of Thunder, Hear My Cry*
by Mildred D. Taylor.

Joyce Carol Thomas.

Brenda Wilkinson.
Photograph by Archie Hamilton.

Camille Yarbrough.

McCannon, Dindga (1947-)
ILLUSTRATOR

McCannon was born in Harlem and studied at the Art Student League and the City University of New York. At seventeen she exhibited her work in a one-woman show, followed by other exhibitions: The PAX Gallery, Genesis II, The Black Expo, and the Harlem Outdoor Art Show. She was co-founder of a black women's art collective, Where We At. McCannon has also worked as a dress designer, teacher of print making, and jewelry designer. She both illustrated and wrote the text for *Peaches*, her first children's book.

Bibliography:

Omar at Christmas by Edgar White. Lothrop, 1973 (o.p.).

Sati the Rastifarian by Edgar White. Lothrop, 1973 (o.p.).

Children of Night by Edgar White. Lothrop, 1974 (o.p.).

Peaches. Lothrop, 1974.

Magubane, Peter (1932-)
ILLUSTRATOR

The photographer was born in Johannesburg. He started his career as a photographer in 1956 on the magazine *Drum* and was a staff member in 1956 of the *Rand Daily Mail*, a Johannesburg newspaper. For more than twenty years Magubane was the only major black South African news photographer. His experiences, recorded in *Magubane's South Africa*, portray his arrests, banning orders, solitary confinement, and other experiences under the apartheid system. He still has a home in Dupkloof, a section of the black township of Soweto outside Johannesburg.

Bibliography:
Black Child. Knopf, 1982.

Mathis, Sharon Bell (1937-)
AUTHOR

Mathis was born in Atlantic City, the daughter of John Willie and Alic Mary [Frazier] Bell. She has taught parochial school in Washington, D.C., was a special education teacher, and was Writer-in-Residence at Howard University. As a member of the D.C. Black Writers Workshop in the early 1970s, she was designated Writer-in-Charge of the children's literature division. Mathis has a bachelor's degree from Morgan State College and a master's in library science from Catholic University of America. Her interviews of children for *Ebony Jr.* magazine are well known. She has been a member of the Black Women's Community Development Foundation since 1973 and is currently a media specialist in the Friendship Educational Center.

Sidewalk Story was the winning manuscript in the Council of Interracial Books for Children writers' contest in 1970. *Teacup Full of Roses* was an American Library Association Notable Book, and *The Hundred Penny Box*, a Newbery Honor Book, now available as a Puffin paperback, was the basis for a children's film. She received a fellowship from Wesleyan University and recognition from the Weekly Readers Book Club and the Bread Loaf Writer's Conference. She won the Coretta Scott King Award in 1974 for *Ray Charles* and the Wallace Johnson Memorial Foundation Award in 1984 for "outstanding contributions to the literary arts." Her memberships include the D.C. Association of School Librarians and Reading is Fundamental.

She lives in Maryland, close to Washington, D.C.

Bibliography:

Sidewalk Story. Viking, 1971.

Ray Charles. Crowell, 1973.

Listen for the Fig Tree. Viking, 1974 (o.p.).

The Hundred Penny Box. Viking, 1975.

Teacup Full of Roses. Viking, 1982.

Meriwether, Louise M. (1923-)
AUTHOR

Meriwether was born in Havestraw, New York, received her bachelor's degree from New York University, and in 1965 received her master's from the University of California in Los Angeles. She has worked as a story analyst at Universal Studios in California, a legal secretary, and a freelance writer, publishing articles and short stories in magazines. Her memberships include the Watts Writers' Workshop, the Authors Guild, and Harlem Writers Guild.

Bibliography:

The Freedom Ship of Robert Small Prentice-Hall, 1971.

Don't Ride the Bus on Monday: The Rosa Parks Story. Prentice-Hall, 1973.

Millender, Dharathula [Hood] (1920-)
AUTHOR

Millender, librarian, teacher, and author, was born in Terre Haute, Indiana, where she graduated from Indiana State University. She has completed additional study at Indiana and Purdue Universities and at Catholic University of America.

Millender was a teacher and librarian in South Carolina and Maryland, a reference assistant at the Library of Congress, a librarian at a Military Reservation, a junior high school librarian in Baltimore and Gary, Indiana. From 1962-1964 and 1966-1967 she chaired Negro History Week Observance in Gary. She wrote the daily column "Yesterday in Gary," edited the *Gary Crusader*, and contributed to *Education and Changing Education*. She has memberships in the American Federation of Teachers, Negro Cultural Achievement Committee, Indiana School Library Association, Indiana State Teachers Association, Alpha Kappa Alpha, and the NAACP.

Bibliography:

Cripus Attucks, Boy of Valor. Bobbs–Merrill, 1965.

Martin Luther King, Jr., Boy with a Dream. Bobbs–Merrill, 1969.

Louis Armstrong, Young Music Maker. Bobbs–Merrill, 1972.

Miller, Don (1923-)
ILLUSTRATOR

The artist was born in Jamaica and grew up in Montclair, New Jersey. He obtained a certificate in art from Cooper Union in 1949 and also attended the New School for Social Research. He has illustrated more than thirty books, magazine articles and film strips. His art has been exhibited at the Museum of Natural History's exhibit "The Children of Africa." His memberships include the National Conference of Artists and the Society of Illustrators.

Bibliography:

The Black BC's. Dutton, 1972.

Jocko: A Legend of the American Revolution by Earl Koger. Prentice-Hall, 1976.

Bicycle From Bridgetown by Dawn Thomas. McGraw-Hill, 1975.

The Creoles of Color by James Haskins. Crowell, 1975.

Langston Hughes, American Poet by Alice Walker. Crowell, 1974.

Moore, Carman Leroy (1936-)
AUTHOR

Born in Lorain, Ohio, the composer received his bachelor's degree from Ohio State University and his master's from Julliard School of Music. He was an assistant professor of music at Yale University and Manhattanville College, a record reviewer and columnist for the Sunday *New York Times*, a music critic for the *Village Voice* and the *Saturday Review*, and a columnist for *Essence* and *Vogue* magazines. Moore was founder and Secretary-Treasurer of the Society of Black Composers. The San Francisco Symphony Orchestra commissioned his composition "Gospel Fuse," and the New York Philharmonic Orchestra commissioned "Wildfires and Field Songs."

Bibliography:

Somebody's Angel Child: The Story of Bessie Smith. Crowell, 1969.

Moore, Emily R. (1948-)
AUTHOR

Moore was born in New York and educated in city schools. At City College of New York she majored in Russian and earned her bachelor's degree, graduating cum laude. She earned her master's degree from Columbia University's Teachers College. Her then unpublished manuscript, "Letters to a Friend on a Brown Paper Bag," was declared a winner of the Council on Interracial Books for Children's seventh annual contest.

Bibliography:

Something to Count On. Dutton, 1980.

Just My Luck. Dutton, 1982.

Musgrove, Margaret [Wynkoop] (1943-)
AUTHOR

Musgrove was born in New Britain, Connecticut, where she attended the local schools. She is a graduate of the University of Connecticut and Central Connecticut State College, where she received her master's degree. She has a Ph.D. in Education from the University of Massachusetts.

The author lived in Accra, Ghana, and has been a English high school teacher in Hartford, Connecticut, a counselor and teacher at Berkshire Community College in Pittsfield, Massachusetts, and Director of Middle College. She is a member of the Society of Children's Book Writers and the League of Women Voters. Her book *Ashanti to Zulu: African Traditions* was a Caldecott Honor Book. A mother of two children, Musgrove lives in Baltimore.

Bibliography:

Ashanti to Zulu: African Traditions illustrated by Leo and Diane Dillon. Dial, 1977.

Myers, Walter Dean 1937-)
AUTHOR

Myers was born in Martinsburg, West Virginia. He speaks of his adoptive parents fondly; the Dean family adopted him informally after his mother's death. He attended City College in New York and received his bachelor's degree in communications from Empire State College in 1984.

In 1981 he received a fellowship from the New Jersey State Council of the Arts, and in 1982 a grant from the National Endowment of the Arts. He is a member of the Harlem Writers Guild, the New Renaissance Writer's Guild, and P.E.N. International. He has written articles for magazines, and was editor of Bobbs-Merrill publishing house. He plays the flute and photography is a hobby.

Although most of his books are about the black experience or have urban settings, a couple of his books have been based on travels to the East and Africa. His book *Motown and Didi* won the Coretta Scott King Award in 1985 as did *The Young Landlords* in 1983. His *Where Does the Day Go*, a prize-winning book, was submitted to Parents Magazine Press in the late 1960s by the Council on Interracial Books for Children. He is married to Constance Brendel and lives in New Jersey with his three children, Karen, Michael, and Christopher.

Bibliography:

Fast Sam, Cool Clyde, and Stuff. Viking, 1975.

It Ain't All for Nothin'. Viking, 1978.

The Black Pearl and the Ghost. Viking, 1980.

Hoops. Delacorte, 1981.

The Legend of Tarik. Viking, 1981.

Won't Know Till I Get There. Viking, 1981.

Tales of a Dead King. Morrow, 1983.
Motown and Didi: A Love Story. Viking, 1984.
Mr. Monkey and the Gotcha Bird. Delacorte, 1984.
Crystal. Viking, 1987.

Palmer, C[yril] Everard (1930-)
AUTHOR

The writer and teacher was born in Kendal, Jamaica, and educated at Mico Training College in Jamaica and Lakehead University in Thunder Bay, Ontario. He has contributed short stories and articles to Jamaica's leading newspaper. Among his awards is a certificate of merit from the Jamaican Reading Association for his contribution to Jamaican children's literature. He teaches and lives in northwestern Ontario.

Bibliography:
The Cloud with the Silver Lining. Bobbs-Merrill, 1966.

Big Doc Bitteroot. Bobbs-Merrill, 1968.

The Sun Salutes You. Bobbs-Merrill, 1970.

Baba and Mr. Big. Bobbs-Merrill, 1972.

A Cow Called Boy. Bobbs-Merrill, 1972.

Patterson, Lillie G.
AUTHOR

Patterson has been a teacher and Chairman of the Elementary Book Reviewing Committee for the Baltimore public school system and a library services specialist. Her book *Martin Luther King, Jr.: Man of Peace* won the Coretta Scott King Award in 1970.

Bibliography:

Frederick Douglass: Freedom Fighter. Garrard, 1965 (o.p.).

Sequoyah: The Cherokee Who Captured Words. Garrard, 1975 (o.p.).

Coretta Scott King. Garrard, 1977.

Sure Hands, Strong Heart: The Life of Daniel Hale Williams. Abingdon, 1981.

David, the Story of a King. Abingdon, 1985.

Petry, Ann [Lane] (1908-)
AUTHOR

Ann Petry was born in Old Saybrook, Connecticut, and attended Connecticut College of Pharmacy, now known as the University of Connecticut School of Pharmacy. She also attended Columbia University.

Her writing career started with her work for the *Amsterdam News* as a writer and reporter, and as Women's Editor in the 1940s for the *People's Voice* a New York newspaper. During 1974 and 1975 she was a visiting professor of English at the University of Hawaii. Her awards include a grant from the National Endowment for the Arts. She married George D. Petry and has one daughter.

Bibliography:

The Drugstore Cat illustrated by Susanne Suba. Crowell, 1949.

Harriet Tubman: Conductor on the Underground Railroad. Crowell, 1955.

Tituba of Salem Village. Crowell, 1964.

Legends of the Saints illustrated by Anne Rockwell. Crowell, 1970.

Pinkney, Jerry (1939-)
ILLUSTRATOR

The artist was born in Philadelphia and educated at the Philadelphia Museum College of Art. An illustrator and designer for many years, Pinkney was involved in design work for the Boston National Center of the Afro-American Artist and a visiting critic for the Rhode Island School of Design.

Pinkney has won several awards for his illustrations, including gold, silver, and bronze medals in the Art Director's Show, and awards from the Society of Illustrators and the American Institute of Graphic Arts. He has also received recognition from the Council of Interracial Books for Children, the National Conference of Christians and Jews, the Carter G. Woodson Book Award, and the New England Book Show, among others. His illustrations for *Patchwork Quilt* by Valerie Flournoy won the 1986 Coretta Scott King Award.

His art projects include record album covers and postage stamps for the United States Postal Service Black Heritage Commemorative Series, principally the Harriet Tubman and Martin Luther King, Jr., stamps. In 1982 he was invited to serve on the United States Postal Service Stamp Advisory Committee, and in 1985 was invited to serve on the Quality Assurance Sub-Committee.

Pinkney resides with his family in Croton-on-Hudson, New York.

Bibliography:

The Adventures of Spider by Joyce Cooper Arkhurst. Little, 1964.

Song of the Trees, by Mildred D. Taylor. Dial, 1975.

Mary McLeod Bethune by Eloise Greenfield. Crowell, 1977.

Childtimes: A Three-Generation Memoir by Eloise Green-field and Lessie Jones Little. Crowell, 1979.

Count on Your Fingers, African Style by Claudia Zaslavsky. Crowell, 1980.

Patchwork Quilt by Valerie Flournoy. Dial, 1985.

Half a Moon and One Whole Star by Crescent Dragon-wagon. Macmillan, 1986.

The Tales of Uncle Remus: The Adventures of Brer Rabbit as told by Julius Lester. Dial, 1987.

Prather, Ray
ILLUSTRATOR

The artist grew up in Marianne, Florida. He studied art at Florida Chipola Jr. College and continued his studies at Cooper Union. He has been an art assistant and designer for *Look* magazine, and his illustrations have appeared in *The Nation* and *Black Enterpsrise*. He lives in Montreal.

Bibliography:

Anthony and Sabrina written and illustrated by Ray Prather. 1973 (o.p.).

No Trespassing. Macmillan, 1974 (o.p.).

Double Dog Dare. Macmillan, 1975 (o.p.).

New Neighbors. McGraw, 1975 (o.p.).

The Ostrich Girl. Scribner's, 1978.

Quarles, Benjamin (1905-)
AUTHOR

Born in Boston, Quarles was educated in local public schools and in 1931 graduated from Shaw University. He is recognized for his knowledge of Afro-American history and scholarly achievements. Quarles earned his Ph.D. in 1940. He was Professor of History and Dean of Instruction at Dillard University and a professor at Morgan State College, where he received fellowships and grants-in-aid from the Social Science Research Council. He also received the President Adams Fellowship in Modern History from the University of Wisconsin, and others from the Rosenwald and Guggenheim Foundations. His affiliation with the Association for the Study of Negro Life and History was productive. He was also President of Associated Publishers and Associate Editor of the *Journal of Negro History*.

Bibliography:

Lift Every Voice with Dorothy Sterling. Zenith Books, 1965.

Robinet, Harriette Gillem (1931-)
AUTHOR

Robinet grew up in Washington, D.C., and recalls childhood summer vacations near the Robert E. Lee mansion in Arlington, where her grandparents had lived as slave children. She received her bachelor's degree at the College of New Rochelle and graduate degrees at Catholic University of America. She worked as a research bacteriologist at Walter Reed Army Medical Center and taught biology at Xavier University.

Her writing began after her family's move to Illinois in 1960. Her children's book is based on personal observations of her son, disabled by cerebral palsy, and many other disabled youngsters she has met. She lives with her husband and six children in Oak Park, Illinois.

Bibliography:

Ride the Red Circle. Houghton, 1980.

Robinson, Adjai (1932-)
AUTHOR

This native of Sierre Leone, Africa, studied at Columbia University. He began collecting folktales from Nigeria and his native country for storytelling on radio in Sierra Leone. His folktale collection and storytelling skills have helped him with his studies at Hunter College and the United States International School.

Bibliography:

Femi and Old Grandaddie illustrated by Jerry Pinkney. Coward, 1972.

Kasho and the Twin Flutes illustrated by Jerry Pinkney. Coward, 1973.

Singing Tales of Africa illustrated by Christine Price. Scribner's, 1974.

Three African Tales illustrated by Carole Byard. Putnam, 1979.

Robinson, Louie, Jr. (1926-)
AUTHOR

Louie Robinson was born in Dallas and attended Jefferson City's Lincoln University. He also served in the Army during World War II. Many of his works were contributed to *Jet, Ebony, Tan,* and *Negro Digest* magazines. He was also an editor for *Jet* and *Romance* magazines and served as *Ebony's* West Coast Bureau Chief.

Bibliography:

Arthur Ashe, Tennis Champion. Doubleday, 1967.

Rollins, Charlemae [Hill] (1897-1979)
AUTHOR

Rollins was born in Yazoo City, Mississippi, and attended Western University, the University of Chicago, and Columbia University, from which she received an honorary doctorate in 1974. She moved to Chicago in 1927. Her attempts to collect materials on blacks revealed that little positive information was available for children. She began collecting material to combat existing stereotypes and was, as a result, instrumental in editing the bibliography *We Build Together*. It was published by the National Council of the Teachers of English in 1963 and revised in 1967. The bibliography defined criteria for selecting literature depicting minorities in a positive light.

Rollins was a well known librarian, children's literature specialist, author, and lecturer. In 1979 she was voted Young Reader's Choice by children in Alaska, Idaho, Montana, Oregon, Washington, British Columbia, and Alberta, in a contest sponsored by The Children's and Young Adult divisions of the Pacific Northwest Library Association. She received the Constance Lindsay Skinner Award of the WNBA in 1970, the Grolier Society Award in 1955, Woman of the Year of Zeta Phi Beta in 1956, the American Library Association Library Letter Award in 1953, and the Coretta Scott King Award in 1971, and was made an honorary member of Phi Delta Kappa.

After working for thirty-six years in the Chicago Public Library, Rollins retired in 1963 as head of the children's room at the George C. Hall Branch. She served as President of the American Library Association's Children's Services Division in 1957–1958, and was a member of the Newbery-Caldecott Committee.

She attributed her love for books to her grandmother, a former slave. A room of the Carter G. Woodson Regional Library was dedicated to her in 1977.

Bibliography:

Christmas Gif'. Follett, 1963.

They Showed the Way: Forty American Negro Leaders. Crowell, 1964.

Famous Negro Poets. Dodd, 1965.

Famous Negro Entertainers of Stage, Screen and TV. Dodd, 1967.

Black Troubador, Langston Hughes. Rand, McNally, 1970.

Ruffins, Reynold (1930-)
AUTHOR/ILLUSTRATOR

The artist was a designer and illustrator for commercial ads and magazines, *Family Circle* among them. He has taught at the School of Visual Arts and Syracuse University's College of Visual and Performing Arts. He has received awards from the Art Directors Club and the American Institute of Graphic Arts, as well as the Cooper Union Professional Achievement Award. He has also received prizes from the Bologna Children's Book Fair in 1976, *California* magazine, the Society of Illustrators, and the New York Historical Society.

Bibliography:

My Brother Never Feeds the Cat. Scribner's, 1979.

If You Were Really Superstitious, by Jane Sarnoff. Scribner's, 1980.

That's Not Fair, by Jane Sarnoff. Scribner's, 1980.

Words: A Book About the Origins of Everyday Words and Phrases, by Jane Sarnoff. Scribner's, 1981.

Salkey, [Felix] Andrew (1928-)
AUTHOR

Salkey was born in Colon, Panama, but grew up in Jamaica. He attended St. George's College in Kingston and Munro College in St. Elizabeth, and earned his bachelor's degree in English from the University of London. He received the Thomas Helmore Poetry Prize in 1955 and a Guggenheim Fellowship in 1960. Salkey taught English in a London comprehensive school and in 1952 became a radio interviewer and scriptwriter for BBC External Services. He married Patricia Verden in 1957 and has two sons.

Bibliography:

Hurricane. Oxford, 1964.

Earthquake. Oxford, 1965.

Jonah Simpson. Oxford, 1969.

Serwadda, William Moses (1931-)
AUTHOR

William Serwadda, son of a Mukanja farmer from the shores of Lake Victoria, was on the faculty of the Department of Music and Dance at Makarerell in Kampala, Uganda. His popular bi-weekly TV program of traditional African music for children received the highest rating. Highly regarded by the Ministry of Culture for his personal musical style, Serwadda was considered a model for his performance of traditional music. Since Uganda's fight for independence in 1962 he has traveled around the country training local clubs interested in preserving traditional music. Serwadda has a master's degree in African studies from the University of Ghana. He has directed choirs in many festivals celebrating African music in his own country as well as Canada, the United States, and Europe. The songs and stories from his book, *Songs and Stories from Uganda*, come from his personal collection of folk material, much of which was acquired in childhood when he lived with his grandfather, an administrator appointed by the king of the Baganda.

Bibliography:
Songs and Stories from Uganda transcribed and edited by Hewitt Pantaleoni. Crowell, 1974.

Shearer, John (1947-)
AUTHOR

Winner of over twenty national awards, this author photographer was born in New York and attended the Rochester Institute of Technology and the School of Visual Arts. His photography has been exhibited in IBM galleries in New York, the Metropolitan Museum of Art's exhibition "Harlem on My Mind," and at Eastman Kodak galleries. Shearer was a staff photographer for *Look* in 1970 and *Life* from 1971–1973 and taught journalism at Columbia University in 1975. He was President of Shearer Visuals in White Plains, New York, from 1980–1984. He produces films featuring characters Billy Jo Jive and Susie Sunset for "Sesame Street."

His *Super Private Eye: The Case of the Missing Ten Speed Bike* won a communications award in 1978. Shearer also received the Ceba Award in 1978 for his animated film, *Billy Jo Jive*. His Billy Jo Jive books, a mystery series for younger readers, are illustrated by his father, cartoonist Ted Shearer.

Bibliography:

I Wish I Had an Afro with illustrations and photographs. Cowles, 1970.

Little Man in the Family with illustrations and photographs. Delacorte, 1972.

Billy Jo Jive and the Case of the Midnight Voices illustrated by Ted Shearer. Delacorte, 1982.

Sherlock, Sir Philip [Manderson] (1902-)

AUTHOR

Born in Jamaica and educated at the University of London as an external student, Sherlock earned his bachelor's degree with first class honors. He has since received an honorary LLD from the University of Leeds and St. Andrews, and honorary doctorates from the University of New Brunswick and Acadia University. He was Vice-Chancellor of the West Indies and was named Knight Commander of the British Empire in 1968. His memberships have included the Association of Caribbean Universities and Research Institutes, the Authors Guild, National Liberal Club, and the West India Club. His principal award was "Commander of the British Empire."

Bibliography:

Anansi, the Spider Man. Crowell, 1954.

West Indian Folk Tales. Oxford, 1966.

Iguana's Tail: Crick Crack Stories from the Caribbean. Crowell, 1969.

Ears and Tails and Common Sense: More Stories from the Caribbean with Sir Philip Sherlock's daughter Hilary. Crowell, 1974.

Steptoe, John [Lewis] (1950-)
ILLUSTRATOR

Born in Brooklyn, the artist attended the New York School of Art and Design, worked with HARYOU-ACT, and studied with painter Norman Lewis. Recognition of his talents began with his first published book, *Stevie*, written and illustrated when he was sixteen and seventeen years old. Among his awards are the Society of Illustrators Gold Medal in 1970, the Coretta Scott King Award in 1981, the Irma Simonton Black Award from the Bank Street College of Education in 1975, and the 1985 Caldecott Honor Book Award for *The Story of Jumping Mouse: A Native American Legend*.

Bibliography:

Stevie. Harper, 1969.

Uptown. Harper, 1970.

Train Ride. Harper, 1971.

All Us Come Cross the Water by Lucille Clifton. Holt, 1973.

My Special Best Words. Viking, 1974.

She Come Bringing Me That Little Baby Girl by Eloise Greenfield. Lippincott, 1974.

Marcia. Viking, 1976.

Daddy Is a Monster . . . Sometimes. Lothrop, 1980.

Mother Crocodile translated by Rosa Guy. Lothrop, 1981.

Outside-Inside Poems by Arnold Adoff. Lothrop, 1981.

All the Colors of the Race by Arnold Adoff. Lothrop, 1982.

Jeffrey Bear Cleans Up His Act. Lothrop, 1983.

The Story of Jumping Mouse: A Native American Legend. Lothrop, 1984.

Mufaro's Beautiful Daughters. Lothrop, 1987.

Sutherland, Efua (1924-)
AUTHOR

"What we cannot buy is the spirit of originality and endeavor which makes a people dynamic and creative." Sutherland, a native of Ghana, a founder of the Ghana Society of Writers, the Ghana Drama Studio, Ghana Experimental Theatre, and a community project called the Kodzidan (the "story house"). She studied at St. Monica's College, Cambridge, and the School of Oriental and African Studies at the University of London. She was a research fellow in literature and drama at the Institute of African Studies, University of Ghana, and is a co-founder of *Okyeame* magazine. Sutherland taught school from 1951-1954, and in 1954 married Afro-American William Sutherland. They have three children and live in Ghana. Sutherland publishes widely in her native land.

Bibliography:

Playtime in Africa, Photographs by Willis E. Bell. Atheneum, 1962 (o.p.).

Tarry, Ellen (1906-)
AUTHOR

The author was born in Birmingham, Alabama. After her arrival in New York, she joined the Writers Workshop at Bank Street College. The Workshop was the brainchild of Lucy Sprague Mitchell, the progressive educator and founder of Bank Street College. Tarry's book *My Dog Rinty*, which grew out of a collaboration with Marie Hall Ets, was popular because of its portrayal of 1940s Harlem. She worked as an Intergroup Relations Specialist with the Department of Housing and Urban Development. Tarry lives in New York.

Bibliography:

My Dog Rinty by Ellen Tarry and Marie Hall Ets. Viking, 1946.

Young Jim: The Early Years of James Weldon Johnson. Dodd, 1967.

Tate, Eleanora Elaine (1948-)
AUTHOR

Tate was born in Canton, Missouri, and raised by her grandmother, Corinne E. Johnson. She graduated from Roosevelt High School in Des Moines and received a bachelor's degree in journalism with a specialty in news editorial from Drake University in 1973.

Her first poem was published when she was sixteen. She started her career as a news reporter and news editor in Des Moines and Jackson, Tennessee. In 1981 Tate received a fellowship in children's literature from the Bread Loaf Writers Conference in Middlebury, Vermont, and in 1982 completed five weeks' travel and research in selected ethnic folk and fairy tales in West Germany and France and in Florence and Collodi, Italy. In 1981 and 1982 Tate was a guest author at the South Carolina School Librarians Association, workshop leader at the 1982 Young Authors Conference, guest speaker at the South Carolina Federation of Business and Professional Women's Clubs' Sixty-Second Annual Convention, and guest speaker at the South Carolina Library Association's annual convention.

Her memberships include the Iowa Arts Council Writers in School program and the South Carolina Arts Commission's artists' roster. She is listed in the Southern Arts Federation's Regional Black Arts Directory. Her book *Just an Overnight Guest* became the basis for a film of the same name produced by Phoenix Films, Inc., New York. She is now co-owner and President of Positive Images, Inc., in Myrtle Beach, South Carolina, and is married to Zack E. Hamlett, III. They have one daughter, Gretchen.

Bibliography:

Just an Overnight Guest. Dial, 1980.
The Secret of Gumbo Grove. Watts, 1987.

Taylor, Mildred D. (1943-)
AUTHOR

Taylor was born in Jackson, Mississippi, but spent her childhood in Toledo, where she attended secondary school and college. After her graduation from the University of Toledo, Taylor joined the Peace Corps in Ethiopia teaching English and history. She became a Peace Corps recruiter upon her return to the United States.

Taylor received a master's degree from the University of Colorado's School of Journalism. As a member of their black students alumni group she helped organize a black studies program and worked as a study skills coordinator.

Her first book, *Song of the Trees*, won the Council on Interracial Books for Children competition, was voted an outstanding book of 1975 by the *New York Times*, and in 1976 was named a Children's Book Showcase book. *Roll of Thunder, Hear My Cry* won the Newbery Medal in 1977 and a nomination for the National Book Award; it was voted a *Boston Globe* Horn Book Award Honor Book and a Notable Children's Trade Book in the field of social studies by the Children's Book Council and the National Council for Social Studies joint committee.

Taylor's Logan family trilogy ended with *Let the Circle Be Unbroken* in 1981. This title was a 1982 American Book Award nominee and a Coretta Scott King Award winner. It was listed among the American Library Association's Best Books for Young Adults in 1981. Taylor resides in Colorado.

Bibliography:
Song of the Trees. Dial, 1975.
Roll of Thunder, Hear My Cry. Dial, 1976.
Let the Circle Be Unbroken. Dial, 1981.
The Gold Cadillac. Dial, 1987.
The Friendship illustrated by Max Ginsburg. Dial, 1987.

Thomas, Dawn C.

AUTHOR

Thomas is a teacher actively involved in the social issues of her New Jersey community. Some of her childhood experiences in Barbados, Harlem, and Brooklyn can be found in her books.

Bibliography:

A Bicycle from Bridgetown illustrated by Don Miller. McGraw-Hill, 1975.

Thomas, Ianthe (1951-)
AUTHOR

Thomas was a nursery school teacher, worked in children's theater, and developed educational curriculum. She studied sculpture at the Universidad de Coimbra in Portugal and has exhibited her wrought iron and milled steel pieces in one-woman shows. Her books are noted for their use of black speech patterns and focus on personal relationships.

Bibliography:

Lordy Aunt Hattie illustrated by Thomas Di Grazia. Harper, 1973.

Eliza's Daddy illustrated by Moneta Barnett. Harcourt, 1976.

My Street's a Morning Cool Street illustrated by Emily A. McCully. Harper, 1976.

Hi, Mrs. Mallory! illustrated by Toulmin-Rothe. Harper, 1979.

Willie Blows a Mean Horn illustrated by Toulmin-Rothe. Harper, 1981.

Thomas, Joyce Carol (1938-)
AUTHOR

Thomas has for many years been known in the San Francisco Bay area for her poetry. The acclaim given her novel *Marked by Fire*, 1983 American Book Award winner in the paperback category for children's fiction, brought her to the forefront as a novelist.

Thomas was born in Ponca City, Oklahoma, almost the middle child in a family of nine. She recalls picking cotton as a child; as an adult she worked as a telephone operator by day while attending night classes, and was, at the same time, responsible for raising four children. She earned her bachelor's degree in Spanish at San Jose University and her master's in education from Stanford University. Among her awards are the Djerassi Fellowship for Creative Artists at Stanford, the Before Columbus American Book Award for her prize-winning novel, *Marked by Fire*, and the Danforth Graduate Fellowship at the University of California at Berkeley. *Marked by Fire* was named a best book by the Young Adult Services Division of the American Library Association and cited as one of the outstanding books of the year, 1982, by the *New York Times*.

Editor of a black woman's newsletter, *Ambrosia*, writer of four plays, and poet of three published volumes, Thomas has lectured in Africa, Haiti, and the United States. She has also served as an assistant professor of black studies at California State University and visiting professor at Purdue University.

Bibliography:
Marked by Fire. Avon, 1982.
Bright Shadow. Avon, 1983.

Walker, Alice (1944-)
AUTHOR

This American Book Award winner for her book for adults *The Color Purple* was born in Eatonton, Georgia, attended Spelman College, and graduated from Sarah Lawrence College. She married Melvyn Rosenman Leventhal and has one daughter, Rebecca Grant.

Walker was a social service case worker for the New York City Welfare Department, a teacher of black studies at Jackson State College from 1968-1969, and Writer-in-Residence at Tougaloo College from 1969-1970. She also designed a course on black women writers, first taught at Wellesley College and later at the University of Massachusetts. Among her awards are the Charles Merrill Writing Fellowship (1967-1968), and the National Foundation for the Arts Award in fiction (1969-1970). She now lives in San Francisco.

Bibliography:

Langston Hughes, American Poet illustrated by Don Miller. Crowell, 1974.

Walter, Mildred [Pitts] (1922-)
AUTHOR

"I came to books late, and later still, to the knowledge that anyone who loves words and applies discipline to that love can create books.

"Being denied access to public libraries and books sharpened my desire to know, not only *what*, but, also *why*. My first opportunity to become a published writer came because I wanted to know why there were so few books for and about the children I taught who were black. "'Write some,' I was told. Write I did out of a need to share with all children the experiences of a people who have a rich and unique way of living that has grown out of the ability to cope and to triumph over racial discrimination.

"My greatest joy is when I see a black child light up when finally there is comprehension that I am the writer, a part of the creation of a book. My having done it, seems to say to him/her, 'She did it, I can, too.'"

Mildred Pitts Walter was born in De Ridder, Louisiana. She is the widow of Earl Lloyd Walter, and the mother of two sons, Earl L. Jr., and Craig A. Walter. She received her bachelor's degree in English from Southern University. Further studies took her to California and Antioch Extension in Denver, where she received her master's in education. She has been a teacher in Los Angeles Unified School District, a consultant at Western Interstate Commission of Higher Education in Boulder, and a consultant, teacher, and lecturer in Metro State College. She devoted most of her time to writing from 1969 on.

Walter has traveled to many parts of the United States and to China and Africa, where in 1977 she was a delegate of the African and Black Festival of the Arts in Lagos, Nigeria. With her husband, who was city chairman of the

Congress of Racial Equality, she also worked with the ACLU and the NAACP toward desegregation in Los Angeles schools. Out of these experiences and her interviews with people during the Little Rock crisis grew the ideas for one of her books, *The Girl on the Outside*. She now lives in Denver.

Bibliography:

Ty's One Man Band illustrated by Margot Tomes. Four Winds, 1980.

The Girl on the Outside. Lothrop, 1982.

Because We are. Lothrop, 1983.

My Mama Needs Me illustrated by Pat Cummings. Lothrop, 1983.

Brother to the Wind illustrated by Leo and Diane Dillon. Lothrop, 1985.

Trouble's Child. Lothrop, 1985.

Justin and the Best Biscuits In the World. Lothrop, 1986.

White, Edgar B. (1947-)
AUTHOR

Born in the British West Indies, the writer came to the United States when he was five years old. He received his bachelor's degree at New York University and completed graduate study at Yale University. His *Underground: Four Plays* and *Crucificardo: Plays* were published by William Morrow and performed at several theaters including the New York Shakespeare Festival Public Theatre and the Eugene O'Neill Foundation. He has written for magazines and the *Yardbird Reader #1*.

Bibliography:

Omar at Christmas illustrated by Dindga McCannon. Lothrop, 1973.

Sati the Rastifarian illustrated by Dindga McCannon. Lothrop, 1973.

Wilkinson, Brenda (1946-)

AUTHOR

Brenda Wilkinson was born in Moultrie and grew up in Waycross, Georgia, the daughter of Malcolm and Ethel (Anderson) Scott and second of eight children. She attended Hunter College of the City University of New York and is a member of the Authors Guild, the Authors League of America, P.E.N. International and the Harlem Writers Guild. *Ludell*, her first book, was a National Book Award nominee in 1976. It was also noted as "Best of the Best" in *School Library Journal*'s listing for 1966–1978. In December 1977, *Ludell and Willie* was voted an outstanding children's book of the year by the *New York Times*, and among the best books for young adults by the American Library Association also in 1977. She is a novelist, short story writer, and poet. Her short story "Rosa Lee Loves Bennie" was included in Sonia Sanchez's anthology, *We Be Word Sorcerers*. She is separated from her husband and lives in New York with her two children, Kim and Lori.

Bibliography:

Ludell. Harper, 1975.

Ludell and Willie. Harper, 1977.

Ludell's New York Time. Harper, 1979.

Not Separate, Not Equal. Harper, 1987.

Wilson, Beth [Pierre]
AUTHOR

Wilson was born in Tacoma, Washington, and graduated from University of Puget Sound, continuing her studies at the University of California in Los Angeles. She was an elementary school teacher in California, a human relations educational consultant, a consultant in creative writing for children and African-American studies in the Berkeley public school system. Wilson has written poems, music, and greeting cards as well as children's books. She has traveled to Africa, Mexico, Canada, Scandinavia, and Hawaii. She is married to a dentist and lives in California.

Bibliography:

Martin Luther King, Jr. Putnam, 1971.

Great Minu. Follett, 1974.

Muhammad Ali. Putnam, 1974.

Giants for Justice. Harcourt, 1978.

Stevie Wonder. Putnam, 1979.

Woodson, Carter Goodwin (1875-1950)
AUTHOR

Woodson was born in Canton, Virginia in 1875. He completed high school when he was twenty-two years old and went on to study at Berea College and the University of Chicago, where he earned both a bachelor's and a master's degree. He earned his Ph.D. at Harvard University in 1912 and then enrolled at the Sorbonne in Paris. He taught elementary and high school, and was a dean of the College of Liberal Arts at Howard University and West Virginia State College.

In 1915 Woodson, described as "the father of modern Negro historiography," organized the Association for the Study of Negro Life and History so that culture and history would be recognized. The *Journal of Negro History* was started when the association was established. *The Negro History Bulletin*, started in 1930, aimed to give school children historical information about their heritage. Woodson's interest in Afro-American history led him to collect documents, write, and compile data on Afro-American roots and heritage.

Bibliography:

African Heroes and Heroines. Associated Publishers, 1938, 1944 (o.p.).

African Myths. Rev. Ed. Associated Publishers, 1948.

Negro Makers of History. Rev. Ed. Associated Publishers, 1948.

Story of the Negro Retold. Rev. Ed. Associated Publishers, 1959.

Yarbrough, Camille (1948-)
AUTHOR

Yarbrough—actress, composer, and singer—has appeared on television and in the theater in a number of roles. She was a member of the New York and touring companies of *To Be Young, Gifted and Black*. *The Iron Pot Cooker*, her recorded songs and dialogues, was favorably reviewed. She was also awarded a Jazzy Folk Ethnic Performance Fellowship by the National Endowment for the Arts. She served as a guest hostess of "Night Talk," Station WWRL, New York, and lecturer at the First World Alliance Net Zion Lutheran Church in New York. Among her awards are: The Unity Award in Media from Lincoln University in 1982 and a "Woman of the Month" citation by *Essence* magazine in 1979. In 1975 she was named "Griot of the Year" by the Griot Society of New York. Born in Chicago and now living in New York, Yarbrough is currently Professor of African Dance in the Black Studies Department of City College of New York, and teaches at African Poetry Theatre, a writing workshop in Queens.

Bibliography:

Cornrows illustrated by Carole Byard. Coward, 1979.
A Little Tree Growing In the Shade. Putnam, 1987.

Young, Andrew Sturgeon Nash [A.S. "Doc" Young] (1924-)
AUTHOR

A.S. "Doc" Young obtained a bachelor's degree at Hampton Institute. He was a sports editor at the *Los Angeles Sentinel*, *Ebony*, *Jet*, and *Hue* magazines. He was also managing editor of *Copper*, *Tan*, and *Jet* magazines and has been a radio commentator. His memberships include the Greater Los Angeles Press Club, Black Economic Union, Publicist Guild, Los Angeles Urban League and the NAACP. Among his awards are the Los Angeles "Ghetto Award," President's Anniversary Sports Award, National Newspaper Publishers Association, and the American Library Association Award for Negro Firsts in Sports.

Bibliography:

Black Champions of the Gridiron: Leroy Keys and O.J. Simpson. Harcourt, 1969.

The Mets from Mobil: Tommie Agee, Cleon Jones. Harcourt, 1970.

Young, Bernice Elizabeth (1931-)
AUTHOR

The author was born in Cleveland and became one of the first of six blacks to be accepted by Vassar College. She has enjoyed writing since childhood, and has worked in advertising for the Beatles. Her other interests include music, ballet, and sports.

Bibliography:

Harlem: The Story of a Changing Community. Messner, 1972.

The Picture Story of Hank Aaron. Messner, 1974.

The Picture Story of Frank Robinson. Messner, 1975.

Young, Margaret B. (1922-)
AUTHOR

Margaret B. Young was the wife of the late Whitney M. Young, Jr., former executive director of the National Urban League. She taught Dr. King's sister at Spelman College and his mother at Atlanta University. She herself majored in English at Kentucky State College, and obtained a master's degree in educational psychology from the University of Minnesota.

Bibliography:

First Book of American Negroes. Watts, 1966.

Picture Life of Martin Luther King, Jr. Watts, 1968.